Pugs

 **W9-ACZ-141**

Dan Rice, D.V.M.

Acknowledgments

My gratitude is extended to the management and editorial staff of Barron's Educational Series, including Editorial Director Kevin Ryan, Acquisitions Editor Wayne Barr, Managing Editor Bob O'Sullivan, and of course Editor Kristen Girardi and Editorial Assistant Hali Chiet for giving me yet another opportunity to pursue my avocation. It is a privilege and pleasure to work with that highly professional group. I would be amiss if I left out my proofreader of this book about Pugs. My wife Marilyn is the most patient and helpful co-worker I could hope for. This book is dedicated to Muggsy the Pug, who was the funniest and most endearing little companion we ever knew.

About the Author

During his many years of small-animal veterinary practice, Dr. Rice found a special place in his heart for Pugs. It was indeed a pleasure to recall, research, and write about this unique breed. His family's Pug (Muggsy) was a castoff that danced and begged her way into the hearts of everyone she met. Researching, reading, and writing this book brought back many joyful memories of the years of Pug ownership. During the past 14 years, Dr. Rice has penned 17 titles for Barron's Educational Series, but none have given him more pleasure than this one.

A Word About Pronouns

Many dog lovers feel that the pronoun "it" is not appropriate when referring to a pet that can be such a wonderful part of our lives. For this reason, the Pug in this book is referred to as "Muggs" and "she" unless the topic specifically relates to male dogs. This by no means infers any preference, nor should it be taken as an indication that either sex is particularly problematic.

Photo Credits
Kent Dannen: pages 10, 12, 19, 20, 23, 24, 27, 34, 39, 41, 43, 45, 70, 73, 77, 105, 106, 115, 121, 122, 126, 129, 135, 138, 146, 153, and 155; Tara Darling: page 162; Cheryl A. Ertelt: pages 3, 8, and 75; Jean M. Fogle: 82, 85, 86, 87, 143, and 151; Karen Hudson: pages 42 and 125; Daniel/Paulette Johnson: pages 58, 96, 97, 98, 99, 100, and 101; Paulette Johnson: pages 4, 6, 9, 14, 16, 28, 30, 37, 44, 46, 48, 49, 51, 52, 54, 55, 57, 59, 64, 67, 69, 79, 80, 91, 93, 108, 112, 117, 132, 136, 140, 145, 147, 148, 154, 156, and 158; Pets by Paulette: pages vi, 7, 32, 60, 63, 95, and 102; Shutterstock: pages i, iii, 2, 5, 18, 31, 35, 88, 139, and 144.

Cover Credits
Shutterstock: front and back cover.

All inquiries should be addressed to:
Barron's Educational Series, Inc.
250 Wireless Boulevard
Hauppauge, New York 11788
www.barronseduc.com

ISBN-10: 0-7641-6226-8 (Book)
ISBN-13: 978-0-7641-6226-8 (Book)
ISBN-10: 0-7641-8678-7 (DVD)
ISBN-13: 978-0-7641-8678-3 (DVD)
ISBN-10: 0-7641-9622-7 (Package)
ISBN-13: 978-0-7641-9622-5 (Package)

Library of Congress Catalog Card No: 2008042375

Library of Congress Cataloging-in-Publication Data
Rice, Dan, 1933–
    Pugs / Dan Rice.
        p. cm.— (Barron's dog bibles)
    Includes bibliographical references.
    ISBN-13: 978-0-7641-6226-8
    ISBN-10: 0-7641-6226-8
    ISBN-13: 978-0-7641-8678-3
    ISBN-10: 0-7641-8678-7
    ISBN-13: 978-0-7641-9622-5
    ISBN-10: 0-7641-9622-7
    [etc.]
    1. Pug. I. Title.

SF429.P9R37 2009
636.76--dc22

2008042375

Printed in China

9 8 7 6 5 4 3 2

CONTENTS

CONTENTS

Purchasing a Pug puppy means a significant investment of money and the beginning of a very long commitment. Those statements aren't meant to discourage the reader from embarking on Pug ownership, but they are facts that you should consider seriously. As a prospective owner, you should choose your canine companion very carefully and select one whose character and attributes blend with your own.

A Pug companion is a touchstone, a living treasure that you will stroke millions of times and cherish for many years. Your Pug is a unique individual that you will never forget, a personality that imprints your life, leaving only happiness in her wake throughout the years you spend together.

Pugs have only one objective in life, and that is to provide the finest companionship available. Pugs catch no mice. They do not guard your estate or frighten away intruders. Since about the first century B.C., Pugs were personal companions to Chinese royalty, Tibetan monks, French and British aristocracy, and more than a few simple sailors and everyday families. They have met that goal for hundreds of years and continue to do so today.

Ownership of a beautiful Pug includes a commitment that is wider in scope than providing doggy necessities and allowing this merry little pet to occupy a portion of your home. Pug ownership is a give-and-take relationship that will continue throughout the little dog's life. That enjoyable companionship thrives when each member of the pair respects the other and camaraderie rules the union. Your Pug will entertain you, love you, and be obedient and faithful to you if you spend time with your doggy friend.

This book focuses on a Pug's unique companionship and behaviors under varying circumstances, and how to discover and enjoy those remarkable traits. It is designed to give you abundant information about your new Pug and offers suggestions to make Pug ownership a pleasant and rewarding experience.

A brief history of canine species is included so that you may better understand hereditary influences on your Pug's personality and behavior. Advice is given to guide readers through puppy selection, getting acquainted, and preparation of your home to accommodate your new companion.

Important information is furnished about your Pug's personality, behavioral modification, and training. Pug activities are introduced, such as obedience, Canine Good Citizens Certification, Therapy Dogs, and conformation shows.

Pug nutrition is included with advice on diet, treats, and dangerous foods. Pug health is discussed in depth, including vaccinations, preventive medicine, hereditary conditions, neutering, and euthanasia.

Browse through this book. Pick a subject you want to learn more about. Then turn to that page to find the answers to your questions.

Chapter One

All About Your Pug's History

Pugs have been around for a long time. They first brought joy to royalty and other dignitaries. In America today, a Pug is the finest companion you can have, regardless of your financial status, position, or importance. A Pug is a little clown that will charm and win you over from the first day you meet her.

A Brief History

Domestic dogs (*Canis familiaris*) are proven by DNA to be progeny of the wolf, *Canis lupus*. Dogs separated from their wolf progenitors about 100,000 years ago and were domesticated about 15,000 years ago. Today, about 400 million domestic dogs of more than 800 pure breeds are living worldwide. More than 50 million dogs live in the United States.

Intelligent prehistoric humans noticed that certain wolf descendents possessed different traits from others in terms of strength, personality, and aptitude. Wolves and their progeny are very malleable and could be encouraged to assist human hunting forays for a share of the prey. Later, other dogs learned to herd and protect humans' flocks. Through selective breeding, different traits were perfected in different dog types. One type developed a talent for catching and killing household pests. Another, because of its large size and ferocity, stood guard over the humans' homes and possessions. Dogs with highly specialized scenting or trailing abilities were in demand by wild game hunters. Later, some lucky dogs were selectively bred to serve their human masters strictly as companions. Pugs, the ultimate companion dogs, originated in the Orient, probably in China and, more specifically, in Tibet about 2,500 years ago.

Muggs is the Pug heroine of this book. She has a twelve-pound body similar in general conformation to an English Mastiff that has been shrunk to lap size. She certainly has the ambition of a big dog, but that aspiration is limited by her physical size. Today's Pug is a tiny dog that packs a lot of fun and enjoyment into a very small parcel. Unlike other toy breeds developed

FYI: Why Dogs?

A recent survey shows that 54 percent of today's dog owners are emotionally dependent on their pets and 59 percent let their dogs sleep with them! Additionally, 82 percent of dog owners said they chose their particular breed for companionship.

Another interesting survey gave the reasons that 19 percent of dog owners are dissatisfied with their dogs.

Complaints included excessive shedding, expense, odors, and nuisance habits. An unexpected reason is that a significant number of those surveyed who were dissatisfied with their dogs had received their pet as a gift or had purchased the pet for their children. Remember that fact when deciding on whether or not you really want a dog.

in the Orient, such as the Shih Tzu, the Lasa Apso, and the Pekingese, the Pug comes equipped with a short coat and straight legs.

Pugs Through the Centuries

The Pug breed originated in the Orient. According to some sources, it dates to 400 B.C. or earlier. Pugs are said to have emigrated first to Japan and later to Europe. They were highly favored companions, playful little dogs that occasionally were bought, swapped, or stolen by sailors on Dutch trading vessels plying the Oriental market places. From there they traveled as shipmates, trade goods, or stowaways from the Orient to the ships' home ports in Holland. From there the Pugs emigrated to other European and Asiatic countries and, eventually, to the New World.

Pugs' names have changed at various times in different countries for different reasons.

- In East China during the Shiang dynasty, Pugs were referred to as Lo-Chiang-Sze or "Foo," which roughly translates as "dragon," possibly because of the bugged eyes of dragons that were depicted in Chinese art of the time.
- In very early Pug books, they were called Dutch Dogs because of their widespread presence and numbers in Holland fairly soon after being developed in the Orient.
- Pugs arrived in Great Britain from Holland no later than the sixteenth century. The name Dutch Mastiff was tagged on them, probably intended

as a compliment because of the similar general appearance to England's Mastiff. The monikers Dutch Pug and Chinese Pug are still commonly used in Great Britain.

- In the pre-Napoleonic era, Pugs arrived in France, where they were known as *Carlin*, which means old hag or witch. In 1790, Napoleon's Josephine owned a Pug named Fortune who played a minor messenger role in the imprisonment of Josephine prior to Napoleon's rise to power. Pugs of France were occasionally depicted in paintings with surgically cropped ears.
- In the Netherlands, Pugs are called *Mopshond* (to grumble).
- The Spanish refer to the Pug as *Dogullo* (translation of name could not be found).
- Italian Pugs are called *Caganlino* (translation of name could not be found).
- In Germany, Pugs are called *Mops*, which may refer to mopish, which means listless or lazy. (Can you imagine a lazy Pug?)
- The Pug's name may be associated with the Pug-faced marmosets that were popular Asiatic pets in about 1700. Those little monkeys' faces do slightly resemble Pug's faces.
- The English translation of the Latin word *pugnua* is "clenched fist," so the Pug's name might have originated because of their rather blunt and rounded faces that somewhat resemble fists.

- In America, we refer to these fun-loving little dogs as Pug Dogs or simply Pugs. The name may be derived from the slang for pugilist, referring to a boxer or prize fighter. Pugs definitely are not fighters, but their pushed-in faces resemble those of cartoon prize fighters.
- The American Kennel Club (the AKC) national breed club of the Pug is formally titled Pug Dog Club of America.

Pug's Place and Time of Origin

If dog breeders kept breeding data in ancient Asiatic cultures, their records have never surfaced. Unfortunately, no AKC was there to formulate and record dogs' pedigrees and times and places of birth. Inhabitants of Oriental castles and monasteries included expert dog breeders who cherished their companion dogs and who were responsible for miniaturizing many of their favorite breeds. Many far-eastern breeds carry their tails tightly curled. A few, like the Pekingese, have heads shaped similarly to the Pug's.

Pugs probably originated in mainland China or Tibetan monasteries in about the first century A.D. In that era, Chinese royalty and Tibetan monks developed several other somewhat similar types and sizes of companion dogs. Like the Pekingese (another breed that came from the Orient),

Breed Truths

The Pug's official motto is a Latin term, *Multum in parvo*, which roughly translates to "a lot in a little." That maxim fits the Pug to a T!

Pugs are of the brachycephalic type, a term that refers to a short muzzle and broad head. Pugs also have tightly curled tails that are carried over one hip. Those features were favored by Oriental breeders. Paintings depicting Pug-like dogs and carvings of similar-appearing Oriental dogs of that period were discovered. Those pieces of art fix those breeds at those times in those regions.

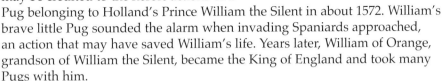
Breed Truths

The actual time and specific locale where the Pug breed was started is unknown because of the lack of recordkeeping at the time the breed was developed.

Pug's Early European Fanciers

Several hundred years after being carried westward from the Orient, Pugs became the highly favored companion pets of Holland's royal families. Much of the Pugs' popularity may be credited to the heroic actions of a Pug belonging to Holland's Prince William the Silent in about 1572. William's brave little Pug sounded the alarm when invading Spaniards approached, an action that may have saved William's life. Years later, William of Orange, grandson of William the Silent, became the King of England and took many Pugs with him.

One German reference suggests that Genghis Khan may have brought the first Pugs to Europe by the seventeenth century. That reference states that the Pug was the pet dog of the nobility, snobs, and old maids.

England's dog shows began during the mid-1800s, and Pugs were first exhibited in 1861. The English studbook began in 1871, and there were sixty-six Pugs in the first volume. Those early Pugs were of a slightly different body structure, and various types were shown that were not necessarily typical of today's Pug.

Black Pugs' Probable Origin

Black Pugs were exhibited in England by their owner, Lady Brasey, in about 1886. Her first black Pug is said to have resulted from a fawn Pug crossed with a Japanese Black Pug. The origin or pedigree of the Japanese Black Pug, to which the reference was made, appears nowhere else in that historical account except to say that the breed was either solid white or black, or a combination of the two colors. Black Pugs of today tend to have small patches of white on their chests or feet. However, information is lacking about why black Pugs typically have single coats instead of double coats like the fawns.

The Pug's Introduction to America

The American Kennel Club was formed September 17, 1884, and the Pug was accepted for AKC registration in 1885. The Pug Dog Club of America was formed in 1931 and was recognized by the AKC that same year. Early American fanciers included Dr. Cryer and his little Pug named Roderick.

Breed Truths

Several tiny breeds known as sleeve dogs were developed in China. They were so called because it was fashionable to tuck those petite canines into dignitaries' ample sleeves and carry them about. However, a sleeve dog was usually of the very smallest variety, and a Pug weighing up to 15 pounds is a bit hefty to carry in a sleeve. Perhaps the earliest Pugs were of a more diminutive size.

American breeders and importers led the Pug's rapidly rising popularity for many years. Pug numbers waned during the 1940s and into the 1950s, at about the time that other toy breeds, such as Pomeranians, Pekingese, and Japanese Spaniels, were being imported in large numbers. Pugs continued to be exhibited in dog shows. During the past 50 years, they have gradually gained in American popularity. It has been said that the Pug is neither so popular to be considered common nor so common to be considered rare.

Probable Progenitors

Little is known of the exact heritage of the Pug. One source of Pug history states that the ancestors of the diminutive Pug may have included the English Mastiff (170 to 190 pounds and about 30 inches tall), but that is problematic. Even if one concedes that Chinese breeders are very adept at miniaturizing their canine favorites, the Mastiff presumably originated in Great Britain and does not have a brachycephalic skull. Additionally, the tremendous size reduction necessary to produce a Pug from Mastiff blood seems highly unlikely.

It seems more likely that Oriental breeds that were available in ancient times were possibly used in Pug development. Those breeds include the aristocratic and sophisticated Pekingese. The Pekingese head type is similar to the Pug's, but the Peke's legs are entirely different in angulation and leg bone structure. Pugs' short, velvety ears and short, flat-lying coats are quite the opposite of the long and feathered coats and long, hairy ears of the Peke. Those facts do not rule out the possibility of one of those breeds being the ancestor of the other. The Shih Tzu was probably developed in the same part of the world at about the same time. Its general appearance is also somewhat similar to the Pug's, but the Shih Tzu coat, leg conformation, and ears, like those of the Pekingese, do not resemble those of the Pug. The question is always the same. Which came first? Pug, Shih Tzu, or Peke?

Reasons for Development

When Pugs reached Holland, it is improbable that they were plentiful or very popular among the general populace because the average canine earned his keep in one way or another. Some were rodent killers for the households or farm granaries; others were setters or retrievers. Many were herding

Fun Facts

Famous Pugs in History

The artist William Hogarth painted a black Pug in about 1730, and several fawn Pugs appear in his other paintings. In several paintings by Goya, Pugs are featured wearing costumes resembling those of royal coachmen.

Lord and Lady Willoughby D'Eresby, Charles Morrison, and Mrs. Laura Mayhew were early English fanciers and breeders. In the mid-nineteenth century, Mrs. Mayhew is recorded to have owned Click, an apricot fawn male that was among the leading sires of English Pugs. Click was sired by Lamb, a dog purchased in Beijing, China. He purportedly was a cross that Mrs. Mayhew needed to produce the desired type and was from pure Chinese bloodlines. An ugly rumor was circulated among the Pug fancy that claimed Click's parents were lemon and white Japanese Spaniels.

dogs, others guarded property, and still others pulled carts. Pugs were designed and bred exclusively for companion roles, and these funny little dogs found their niche among Holland's royalty.

Soon after being seen in Holland, Pugs were found elsewhere in continental Europe, Asia, and Great Britain, where they were also upper class favorites. Throughout Victorian times, Pugs captured the fancy of royalty. They remained greatly desired and were special companions in the historical accounts of the wealthy and famous. When they crossed the Atlantic, where true royalty was absent, their appeal was to the general public as family companions. In that role, no one has ever made a case for their value in any other capacity. In the United States, Pugs were never intended to rid homes of vermin and are useless as pointing or retrieving dogs. (Pugs do, however, have a good sense of smell, proven by their attraction to all kinds of gourmet cooking.) They can't run very far or fast and are too small to be working dogs. A Pug work? You must be kidding!

American Pug owners will tell you that their little four-legged companions rarely carry their weight in marketable endeavors. That doesn't change the fact that Pugs are among the best loved and most excellent canine companion dogs to be found. Almost daily, people from all backgrounds and of all ages are discovering the joy of happy, good natured lap dogs. Among senior citizens, abundant surveys show that owning a lap dog is second only to drinking from the fountain of youth.

The future of Pugs is bright. The 2007 AKC litter registration data lists Pugs as the 13th most popular breed (12,421 litters registered), compared to 25th (6,524 litters registered) in 1989. The registered litters have nearly doubled in the past nine years. The popularity of Pugs keeps increasing although they are not in the top ten. However, Pugs are here to stay!

A Unique and Entertaining Companion

I was a small animal veterinarian in a semi-rural community, and I frequently examined the local shelters' unwanted pets. One day, the dog warden brought in a Pug. She was like many other middle-aged, unwanted, but healthy, happy, affectionate dogs except for one fact. She was about 60 days pregnant.

The chubby little scamp scurried across my waiting room, into the exam room, and sat straight up on her flat bottom before me. Her enormous abdomen and full mammary glands were incongruously balanced on the floor in front of her. She waved her forefeet up and down, searching my soul with her wide, dark, pleading eyes as if to say, "Here I am. Glad to meet you. Now let's go home."

Like most veterinarians I know, I was a sucker for soft eyes. Our family frequently fostered cast-off dogs to board with us until new homes could be found. I chuckled and quickly agreed to help the pathetic little Pug. She presented us with four fat, little, mixed breed puppies two days later. My plans to spay her and find her a new home after she weaned her puppies

didn't work out. Long before the litter was weaned, she was firmly ensconced in our hearts and home.

She was a terrific traveler and went virtually everywhere we went. While traveling on someone's lap or in her crate, she never complained. She tried to follow our boys on their horses a few times, but her legs and breath were too short. She tired quickly and gave up on that endeavor. We enjoyed her clowning presence at all family functions, short and long trips, camping, fishing, and picnicking. She is sorely missed, but she lived a full and happy life.

Several facts set Pugs apart.

Fun Facts

In ancient history, dogs were required to serve useful functions wherever they were found. Companion pets were uncommon.

- They accept everybody, friends and strangers alike, but are loyal companions.
- Pugs are sturdy little dogs and the largest of the AKC Toy Group.
- They are durable, with few health problems if purchased from competent breeders and handled appropriately.
- Pugs are long-lived companions; the average life span is about 15 years.
- They are fun-loving dogs that enjoy entertaining their families.
- Pugs are quite trainable, and you can teach them many tricks if you don't expect miracles.
- They are clean little dogs and easy to housebreak.
- Pugs crate easily and are good traveling companions.
- Most Pugs rarely bark because of their upper respiratory anatomy.

Pugs are far from delicate, but certain shortcomings of the breed must be recognized.

- Pugs' coats are short and easily maintained, but you must have the time to groom them regularly to minimize shedding.
- Perhaps Pugs' major health problems are related to their head conformation. Brachycephalic dogs are all susceptible to heatstroke and respiratory problems when exercised excessively.
- Pugs are voracious eaters and predisposed to obesity.
- Pugs' short muzzles sometimes cause snoring, air swallowing, and flatulence.

Popularity Problems

Everyone wants to own a winner, especially when the winner is as cute as a Pug! Pugs have starred in movies such as *Milo and Otis, Homeward Bound,* and *Pocahontas I* and *II*. Those and many other fantastic little Pugs are occasionally seen on popular TV shows and movies. There is no doubt they helped move Pugs' popularity gradually upward. Those Pug stars of American media are carefully selected and trained by the best canine trainers in the business. Trainers stand on the set, just out of the camera's field of vision, and direct the actions of the canine actors. Not every Pug is as intelligent or as trainable as those canine stars. If not properly managed by her owners, trainers, and handlers, a Pug may never succeed in Hollywood. However, she may perform at birthday celebrations, house parties, and hoedowns.

Great popularity often spoils a normal, healthy breed. Money-grubbers all want to get in on the action. Backyard breeders and puppy mills breed every dog that faintly resembles a Pug, hoping to cash in on a craze. The entire breed is adversely affected by hereditary deformities that are allowed to creep into and dominate the breed by ignorant breeders who want to make a quick buck producing inferior puppies.

Reputable and professional Pug breeders are easily found, but they rarely, if ever, become rich and famous. However, their achievements are quite noteworthy and essential to the maintenance and improvement of the Pug breed. They are the stars in the Pug's crown.

Breed Truths

Anthropomorphism

Anthropomorphism means attributing human characteristics to an animal. We must all recognize that most Pugs display a nearly humanoid personality. Something mystical occurs when your Pug is sitting on your lap or by your chair, waiting to be stroked, looking quizzically at you with her big, sorrowful eyes that make you wonder what, if any, human-like thoughts are running through her brain. She may be trying to coax you to get up and begin playing games. She might instead be planning to entertain you with her humorous antics. Maybe nothing but a vacuum lurks behind those pleading eyes, but a Pug can add joy to your life and improve your health.

Chapter Two

The Mind and Body of a Pug

E xpect the unexpected from your Pug puppy. Muggs will always be ready to go like a windup toy, so you will need boundless patience and an enormous sense of humor. Owning a Pug is like living with a circus clown—there's never a boring moment or a serious thought. However, you must never lose your temper.

Inborn Character

Character means a distinctive trait, attribute, or quality. Pugs are loaded with character! Pugs of any age are funny! A litter of five-week-old Pug puppies are so laughable, so energetic, and so enchantingly clumsy that they will entertain you for hours. Even the way they sleep in piles is humorous. It's difficult to keep your hands off those sad-eyed, chubby little balls of wrinkled fur. Pug puppies grow up quickly, but they never stop being clowns. All their lives they are cute! Why would anyone want to invest time and hard earned money on a few pounds of cuteness? Companionship must have more to offer than cuteness!

Muggs has many admirable, honorable innate features, among which is intelligence mixed with a terrific sense of humor. A Pug is said to be trainable, or quick on the uptake, meaning she's a fast learner. Your Pug will grasp stunts quickly and remember them forever. Teaching tricks to Muggs is usually as easy as offering her a treat. A Pug often will make an amateur trainer shine like a professional, but don't be overconfident. It might be your luck that she will require more training time than you expect, and you must be patient.

Muggs will often astonish you with her ability to recognize emphasized words used in training. Give a command, and she will do something. That something may not be what you had in mind, but it will make you laugh at the very least. If you do laugh out loud, Muggs will probably appreciate your approval and embarrass you by repeating her actions at odd times, proving the notion that Pugs do have a sense of humor.

Pug Personality

Personality refers to behavior, habits, and mental nature. Muggs' charming disposition is not unique to her breed, but she is endowed with more than her share of desirable qualities. Chief among them is her motivation to please her family. A Pug's mission in life is to entertain everyone, all the time.

You may be angry for a second when Muggs raids your popcorn dish during your momentary trip to the kitchen to refresh your iced tea. When you return and see her woebegone, ashamed countenance, your anger will leave, and you will forgive her immediately. You won't even raise your voice or shake your finger and declare that she is a bad dog, because all she did was act naturally. You may even pat her on the head or rub her lovingly when she looks up at you sheepishly, seeking sympathetic understanding. Such is the manipulative personality of a Pug. (Who is the boss?)

Breed Truths

Pugs cheat! It isn't fair for them to have sad eyes and a comical expression to use on you when you are trying to scold.

Muggs is happy with her world whether her roommates are paupers or kings. Her cheerful exuberance fills the room and is appreciated by her human associates, bringing laughter to everyone at regular intervals. Her outgoing personality gives a new meaning to taking a walk in the park or going to the store in your car. She enjoys being with you at all times in all situations. Even though her presence doesn't physically aid you, she makes the simplest task more enjoyable.

CHECKLIST

A Pug's Needs

✔ A kind, considerate, affectionate, and appreciative owner

✔ A soft, warm bed, preferably in your bedroom (not necessarily on your bed)

✔ Clean dishes, two regular meals per day, and fresh water at least once daily

✔ A reward for each task performed, but not necessarily an edible treat

✔ A kennel or crate that doubles for a den and car carrier that she can sleep in when tired

✔ A yard to play in or if not possible, three or four short walks outside per day

✔ Regular grooming, daily if possible, or at least every two or three days

✔ Regular, preventive health care

A Pug's dignity is generally hidden behind her comic attitude and joyful outlook on life, but a grain of decorum is generated on certain occasions. For instance, a few months ago, a Pug in a televised dog show assumed a stance of sedate pride and propriety. Amid much applause, the elegant little Pug stood on the judge's table, majestically, like a Michelangelo sculpture, to receive her hard earned purple ribbon. As the official leaned over to shake her owner's hand, the Pug's ample tongue shot out and wiped the smile from the judge's face. She then began wriggling from stem to stern and brought down the house. Even the judge laughed out loud.

Pugs' Less Known Attributes

Pugs' credits are many and varied. These little guys are easily trained, obedient, responsive, and appreciative of your attention. Because they have never learned to pucker like a human, they kiss their human kin with busy pink tongues. They never hold a grudge when you feed them an hour later than usual, and forgive you for excluding them from your trip to the movies. They can tell time, almost to the minute, and will remind you when suppertime has arrived. Of course, they may give you the same signals for a midday snack if they think they can get away with it.

Sensitive Souls

In case you find yourself totally enamored by your little Pug, one trait should be made clear. A Pug is a gentle, fine-tuned companion. She can have her feelings hurt fairly easily. If you lose sight of that fact and abuse this emotional trait, you may lose your little Pug's invaluable trust. Great sensitivity is a feature of many Pugs, and failure to recognize that peculiarity will likely be irreversibly imprinted in your clownish Pug's hard drive. Pugs were developed with a singular purpose, to be a human companion and

must be treated as such. Your Pug lives with you and for your pleasure, but she must always be treated kindly and gently.

Pugs' hammy and soulful personalities make them excellent therapy dogs. They love to entertain anyone who will participate and who appreciates their sense of humor! Conclusive evidence supports the theory that sharing a home, stroking, caring for, and talking to a companion pet is soothing to human nerves and increases the pleasure of a sometimes lonely existence. The presence of a Pug improves the quality of life for senior citizens and is an excellent pet for a disabled individual who has a small fenced backyard or patio or who has the ability to take a short walk several times a day. Muggs is small, lightweight, easily handled on lead, and not aggressive. Most Pugs never meet a stranger. Even as a puppy, Muggs will recognize friendly neighbors with glee and wriggle her posterior when she meets an agreeable soul, whether or not the person is already known to her.

Pug Characteristics

Muggs' colors and coat are standard issue. Pugs aren't showy but are natural in nearly every aspect. Muggs won't need constant combing to remove tangles and mats. However, she probably isn't a good choice for anyone if persnickety family members can't overlook an occasional Pug hair in their soup or hate to brush their clothes before leaving for work. If a family is in search of a dog to leave out in the backyard all day or wants to take their companion duck hunting, on long hikes, and on biking trips, a Pug is out. Look elsewhere if seeking a guard dog. A Pug is everyone's friend (including a neighborhood burglar). She is great fun and will be a minimal stress on the family income. Her health care and dog food bills are relatively small, and she occupies a minimal amount of space. Muggs does fine in an apartment, but she takes a certain amount of your personal time. She isn't demanding but must have plenty of interaction with her owners. If you can't dedicate a regular portion of your day to playing with and caring for Muggs, buy a nice goldfish instead.

Pug's Description

This paraphrased breed standard is not the official AKC document. It includes numerous additions, comments, and opinions. It is meant to be more descriptive to the novice Pug owner than the Pug Dog Club of America's breed standard.

Muggs' body should be very square and sturdy. Long legs and thin or lean bodies are not desired. Rangy Pugs of that description are commonly found in litters of backyard breeders and puppy mills. Stay away from those places. Don't consider a stumpy puppy with Bassett-like legs that appear too short for her body. Such Pug puppies may be AKC registered. Even though their conformational faults are objectionable, they aren't disqualifying.

For the Pug, one size fits all. Fortunately, the idea of a miniature or teacup-sized Pug hasn't been endorsed by breeders. The Pug remains the same size it has been for many decades. Teacup-sized toy breeds that are purposely inbred for size alone usually carry more genetic disabilities than they can handle and, more often than not, are inferior and weak pets. It would be a shame and a serious error for anything less than standard size to be sanctioned or supported by any registry.

Muggs' overall form should be compact with tightly knit proportions. Her muscles should be firm and solid. She should stand about 10 to 11 inches tall, measured from the floor to the top of her shoulder blades (withers). Although Muggs' weight is not mentioned in the official standard, she should weigh between 14 and 18 pounds and should have the allover appearance of being square. That is, her height from floor to withers should be equal to the length from the foremost point of her breastbone (sternum) to her tail set.

Breed Truths

Black Pugs are rare. They have no appreciable undercoat and are said to shed less, although that is problematic. All Pugs shed profusely.

Head Skin wrinkles are the primary feature seen when Muggs' head is viewed from the front. Her head should appear large, massive, and roundish. It should not resemble an apple sitting on a table. Her face should be blunt when viewed from the side. Her short, square muzzle should not appear upturned, and her skull should have no apparent indentation.

Muggs' eyes are dark, large, prominent, and globe shaped. When viewed carefully, they should have a soft and worried appearance. Her jet black ears are small, thin, and soft. They have the feel of velvet. They are positioned widely and are of two types. Button ears are the preferred type. They bend so the fold is level with the top of her skull, with the tips hanging no lower than the corners of her eyes. Rose ears are smaller, with the edge of their folds held tightly against her skull. Head wrinkles are large, deep, and darker at their depths than on the surface. Her bite should be very slightly undershot but not so much that her teeth show.

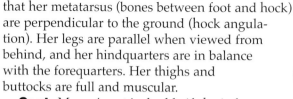
Breed Truths

Black Pugs bred to fawns often produce puppies with undesirable smutty or smoky color.

Neck, Topline, and Body Muggs' neck is slightly arched and blends well with her head and body. It is thick, has the appearance of strength, and should be long enough to carry her head proudly. Her short back is level from the withers to the rump, with a high tail set. Her chest appears wide when viewed from the front, and her overall body appearance is short, thick, and sturdy. Her tail is her trademark. It should be curled as tightly as possible (a double loop is preferable) and carried over one hip. A loosely carried or droopy tail carriage is not desired.

Forequarters Muggs' legs are very strong, straight, of moderate length, and positioned well under her body. When viewed from the side, her elbows are directly under her withers and her shoulder blades are moderately laid back (shoulder angulation). Her pasterns (ankles) are strong, angulated slightly—neither straight up and down nor weak and flattened. Her feet are neither long, like rabbit feet, nor round like those of a cat. Her toenails are black, and her dewclaws are usually removed without anesthesia when she is less than a week old.

Hindquarters Muggs has strong, powerful hindquarters. Her stifles (knees) are moderately bent (stifle angulation). Her hocks (hind leg joint corresponding to the human ankle) bend backward so that her metatarsus (bones between foot and hock) are perpendicular to the ground (hock angulation). Her legs are parallel when viewed from behind, and her hindquarters are in balance with the forequarters. Her thighs and buttocks are full and muscular.

Coat Muggs' coat is double if she is fawn colored. Her guard (outer) hair is longer than the hair of her undercoat and is straight, fine, smooth, soft, and glossy, neither hard nor woolly. Her undercoat is shorter, softer, and somewhat fluffier.

Colors and Markings Most Pug colors are fawn, but black Pugs are available. In either case, Muggs' muzzle or mask is black, and the wrinkles that extend from the muzzle upward on her head are deep. The deeper aspects of fawns' wrinkles are darker colored than the coat over the remainder of the body. Her ears, eyelids, and eyebrows are black. A black or dark line of hair (trace) extends along her spine from her occiput (hindmost point of the skull) to her tail. A fawn's color should be well-defined and should contrast strongly with her black muzzle and her trace. Black moles may be seen on her cheeks as well as a thumb mark or diamond on her forehead. Those markings should also be distinctly defined.

CAUTION

Pugs are sensitive creatures that can be cowed or intimidated and may bite if abused or afraid of their handler.

Some breeders and fanciers prefer "silver fawn, stone fawn, peach fawn, cream," and perhaps other variations of the basic fawn color, but those are mostly personal preferences. Sometimes fawns have a slightly darker appearance because of black-tipped guard hair. If that body coloration is general and quite noticeable, its smutty appearance makes the Pug undesirable to fanciers.

Gait When viewed from the front, a Pug's forelegs are carried well forward, showing no weakness in the pasterns. Her paws should land squarely with the central toes pointing straight ahead. Her rear leg action should be

strong and free through hocks and stifles, with no twisting or turning (pad-dling) in or out. Her hind legs line up with the front, and a slight natural convergence of the limbs is seen in both front and back. A slight roll of her hindquarters typifies the gait, which should be free, self-assured, and jaunty.

Temperament Temperament is rarely criticized in a Pug. Muggs is almost sure to be an even-tempered companion, exhibiting friendliness, stability, playfulness, great charm, and an outgoing, loving disposition. Her clownish habits and fun-loving spirit endear her to the entire family. Pugs aren't known for their aggressiveness toward humans or other animals. Somewhere, at some time, someone was probably attacked and bitten viciously by a Pug, but I've never seen or heard of such an event. Some Englishmen nicknamed the Pug "Chinese Mastiff" at one time in history. Probably that oxymoron was not referring to the Pug's temperament but was jokingly referring to the paradoxical size difference and conformational similarity of the two breeds' bodies.

Expression Muggs probably has the most charming personality of any dog you have met. Much of her appeal is caused by her expression. Her big dark eyes, muzzle wrinkles, laughable appearance, and tail action are discussed in a clinical, matter of fact manner, but you must truly study your Pug's expression before you realize that you are hooked. You may never get beyond her engaging expression.

Friendliness The reason for Pug pets is simple. People like tiny dogs that are fun to be around. Pugs are favorites with children because kids like Pugs and Pugs like kids. Grownups are fascinated by the sense of humor possessed by Pugs. Muggs' sociability is almost as important to adults as her laughable countenance and habits. For those reasons, she is simply a wonderful companion.

Hereditary Pug Behavior

Muggs is a special dog in the finest meaning of the term, but her progenitors were wolves. If observed closely, a domesticated and well-socialized Pug may exhibit a few characteristics that are shared with wolves. Those traits include territorial marking, defending her den, circling before she lies down, scratching to cover her feces or urine, and respect for the alpha leader of her pack.

Dogs are quite malleable. Humans exploited that quality to modify a number of breeds that are listed in the AKC Toy Group. Many of those little canines possess lightning quickness and independent thinking.

Muggs the pup is cute, cuddly, and sometimes demanding, but she is always fun. She has a gigantic ego hidden under her slick coat, but her play is not usually offensive or destructive. She will wear herself out playing, sleep until she is refreshed, rise, eat (if anything is offered), and continue her play. She may chew anything found lying on the floor. She eats voraciously and is naturally clean and very trainable. However, she was not housebroken at birth. Her tiny stature may dominate her natural self-important attitude. Sometimes a tiny Pug puppy becomes timid because she realizes that even a child is much larger, stronger, and sometimes overwhelming.

Marking

Hunting and killing their food and marking their territory was, and still is, the prerogative of feral canines such as the wolf, coyote, or fox. Likewise, a domestic male canine marks his territory to warn other males that he was here first and to tell females that he is available in case need arises. The urine of a canine female has a definite odor when she is in season, informing male canines that the young lady is ready for romance.

You have no doubt witnessed male dogs marking trees and bushes by heisting one hind leg and squirting a bit of urine on the vertical surface. On her first few leashed walks, Muggs will be more interested in squirrels and birds than investigating doggy odors that abound outdoors, especially in uncharted regions. When she is a little older, she will stop at each post and clump of flowers to sniff and mark. Oh yes, a female dog, even a spayed female, marks her territory, although you may have never seen her do it. She is a spayed female and has nothing to advertise, but the wolflike instinct remains. She will mark the area she inhabits if she gets the chance. Some experts claim that urinary markings will give her touchstones to help her find her way back to her den, and that may be true.

PERSONALITY POINTERS
Pug Body Language

Pug Mood	Friendly	Curious or Excited	Playful
Head Carriage	Very animated with anxious movement from side to side	Tipped first to one side then to the other	Sometimes bowed with elbows bent, sometimes alertly seeking action or toys
Eyes	Wide open, expectant with excited anticipation	Wide open and darting from side to side, actively seeking the action	Wide open, darting from one thing to another
Ears	Twitching slightly, almost unnoticeably	Twitching slightly	Twitching slightly
Mouth	Open with tongue out, maybe grinning, ready to lick a face if one presents itself	Wide open and panting rapidly, perhaps drooling	Open and closed intermittently
Body	Wriggling all over, very animated	Wriggling vigorously	Wriggling at both ends
Tail	Tightly curled, carried over one hip, usually wagging and animated	More vigorous wagging	Wagging incessantly

Circling

Muggs may sometimes circle for a few seconds immediately before she lies down. That is an inherited characteristic of all canines and one that may have any number of reasons. It was probably originally done to pack down the tall grass and provide a soft sleeping nest that was less visible to predators. Some say it was to carefully sniff the nesting area to be sure no other animal had already established site ownership.

Mouthing

Mouthing is a natural puppy trait. Some people believe that Muggs is putting her mouth on an object to help her teething process. If the object being mouthed is a firm, chewable object, that may be true. However, mouthing is a Pug's method of tasting virtually everything in her

Helpful Hints

Remember, you are in charge. You are the alpha leader of the pack. You own the Pug; she doesn't own you, regardless of how it appears!

Apprehensive or Anxious	Fearful	Subordinate
Straight forward and slightly bowed	Head is resting on forefeet in front of body, under the bed	Slightly lowered
Wide open but quiet, more soulful appearing than usual	Possibly looking upward toward your face	Open with a soft squint
Drooped slightly	Probably normal for a recumbent position	Flattened against the head
Closed tightly (seen very rarely)	Hard to see because she is under the bed	Closed because she is belly-up
Lying down, head on feet	Prone and under the bed	Belly-up in front of you
Wagging at a slower pace	Only slightly wagging and totally stopped on occasion	Still curled tightly but lying under body or on hip

environment. Muggs sees an interesting object, picks it up, and remembers how it tastes. Rocks and leaves are generally tasted only once because they fail to please her discerning palate. A child's sneaker is different because it tastes like leather or plastic that is quite agreeable. More importantly, she likes shoes and socks because they carry the taste of her playmates.

Mouthing is not a bad habit but chewing is the next step, and that must be controlled. Muggs never chews maliciously. She tastes, and sometimes chews, shoes, belts, shirt cuffs, book spines, electric cords, the corners of furniture, doors, and just about any other object that she can grip in her tiny needle-like teeth. A five-pound puppy can cause a great deal of damage in a very short time, but chewing is a bad habit that can be controlled. (See *Training*, page 66.)

Licking

Muggs loves you and your family. She spends a lot of time in close relationship with you for many reasons. Her affection for her human counterparts is demonstrated by licking. Muggs' mother licked her face, and each puppy licked the face of its siblings as well. So why should she not want to lick your face? You can stop the licking habit by scolding, but that is a mistake. Under normal circumstances, it is doubtful that any harmful germs will be transferred to you or your children by Muggs licking a few chins. Sometimes you must be quick in order to avoid a busy tongue across your lips, but that should improve your reflexes next time.

If you honestly think it necessary to initiate a possible solution to the "problem" of unwanted licking, try telling Muggs in a normal voice, "No lick" or "Enough licking." Immediately after issuing one of those commands, gently push her head away or put her on the floor. Please don't damage your relationship with your sensitive little Pug by sternly reprimanding her or, heaven forbid, by swatting her with your hand.

Barking

Your Pug very likely will not be a good burglar alarm. Just in case Muggs tends to bark a lot, that vice should be addressed. Her barking probably will be directed at the front door, where she will frighten the dangerous mail carrier or the package delivery person. That habit is easily understood when you look at the situation from a dog's viewpoint. The person being barked at wears a uniform, comes to your door, rattles the mailbox, or rings the bell. When Muggs barks at that intruder, the noisy person quickly scurries away. Thus, in her thoughts, the delivery person was trying to break in and when Muggs, the brave little Pug, barked, the intruder was frightened away. Can you expect anything different from her next time? Excessive and repeated barking is an irritating nuisance. It can be partially controlled with simple verbal commands (*come, sit, stay*). However, yelling at Muggs is a mistake. A sensitive Pug will never understand why you yell her name every time she has everything under control.

Pack Superiority

If more than one dog lives in a family, the dogs form their own society or pecking order. Usually the oldest dog will assume the dominant or alpha role in the pack, because she or he has more experience than the younger ones. Pug pack roles usually take a backseat to having fun, and each of the dogs of the family acts equal to all others. This may or may not be the case in your home. If you own several dogs of any size or breed, you may experience situations in which one member of the canine pack wants to take the leadership role. The alpha dog may be either male or female. That dog will exert the leadership role with a sharp bark and a snap of teeth. The recipient of the reprimand immediately backs down. This is normal behavior, and you shouldn't interfere with it unless the scrapping is happening regularly or one dog is actually injured by another.

Body Language

Body language is well developed in all dogs, and Pugs are no exception. Wrinkling your forehead, squinting your eyes, and frowning will very likely bring a guilty look to Muggs' face. She is probably responding to what she believes to be a domineering posture. She doesn't realize that you are actually frowning because she accidentally tipped over a vase of flowers an hour ago. In other words, unless you actually see what is happening and can respond immediately, don't bother to act angry. Don't scold, or heaven forbid, strike Muggs for something that happened when you weren't present.

10 Questions on Pug Behavior

1 **We live on a rural acreage and need a mouser. Is the Pug a good choice for us?** A Pug isn't an animated mouse trap because she wasn't designed for that purpose. She will probably ignore a rodent or try to play with it because Pugs have no innate "killer instinct." If you can teach her to catch a mouse, she might obey once. It is unlikely that she will seek and destroy all helpless little field mice. Buy a small terrier.

2 **My wife and I are outdoors people, and we want a little dog to enjoy our lifestyle. Is that a good life for a Pug?** It depends on how far you hike, how rough and dusty the trails might be, and the outside temperature. A Pug isn't a weakling or without stamina, but her head and upper air channel are incompatible with dusty trails. Short-legged brachycephalic Pugs do not tolerate hot summertime temperatures and long walks without shade.

3 **Is a Pug a good apartment dog?** A Pug can get plenty of exercise just keeping up with you and entertaining you when you aren't busy. The size of the apartment isn't the determining factor; it is the amount of time you are available. If you have time to take your pug out several times a day for toilet breaks and perhaps to a nearby park once a day for an evening walk, Muggs will be a great choice. If you set aside grooming time several evenings a week and also training and play sessions almost every day, your Pug should never become bored or melancholy.

4 **We don't want a shy Pug that doesn't mix well with strangers. Where can we find a well-socialized one?** Timidity is not a Pug trait. Of course, exceptions do exist. To be quite sure, consult your breeder. A good, competent Pug breeder will socialize all puppies when they are quite young. He or she will watch the puppies and pick out one for you that is strong, slightly aggressive, robust, and playful.

5 **How can I train my next dog not to bark?** A Pug is generally not a good burglar alarm because some never bark. A few do bark at the doorbell, but a barking vice is not a major concern. To control inappropriate barking when guests arrive, put your Pug's treat jar on the table. Ask one or more of the guests to call your Pug and offer her a small treat every 10 or 15 minutes. That technique may be used with those who arrive unexpectedly at your door also. Keep the treat jar beside the door, and ask the person to give your Pug a treat as soon as you open the door. A Pug that is greeted at the door with a tidbit usually accompanies the guest, looking for more. Giving a few treats at intervals usually quiets the Pug who loves treats and doesn't like to bark anyway. Thus, the Pug makes a new friend with treats and will usually watch for that person to return with his treat jar sans barking.

6 **Why do all small dogs lick? Face licking is disgusting! How can I stop it?** Pugs lick because it is physically impossible for them to pucker up and kiss. They lick faces because they are taught to do so by their mothers. Kissing or face licking is inherently a natural greeting, not a vice. It is an affection exhibition, and it is reserved for those whom the dog loves and wants to be near. If you scold your Pug for licking, you may discourage the habit. You are also sending a message along with your scolding, a message that says, "Don't love me! Get away from me!" If that is your intent, I'd suggest investing in a cat or goldfish.

7 Our last Pug chewed up my most expensive shoe. How can I stop chewing? Puppies put their mouths on objects to taste them. Your shoes have your own personal body odor and taste, and your Pug recognizes it. Tasting your shoe with her tongue isn't malicious, but chewing may follow tasting. The best way to stop your Pug from chewing is to keep personal items out of your Pug's reach.

8 A friend had a small dog that had to be given up because of a condition called separation anxiety. What is that all about? Is it common in Pugs? Can it be prevented? Separation anxiety in a Pug is rarely encountered but is possible. It doesn't spontaneously erupt. The pattern slowly builds and is associated with the dog's instinctive desire to be with her family. The syndrome progresses from boredom to nervousness, panic, urination, defecation, chewing up virtually everything in sight, and generally trashing the house. It is best controlled by leaving for work without fanfare. Don't rattle your car

keys, and don't say good-bye. Crating can be used and often works well. Hollow, food-containing toys often help, and frequent absences for short periods are important.

9 Why does my Pug turn around and around before she lies down? Circling before lying down is a behavioral characteristic of all canines, inherited from wolf ancestors. Circling was possibly done to pack down the tall grass and provide a soft sleeping nest that was screened from predators, or it was done to sniff the nesting area to be sure no other animal had already established site ownership.

10 I take walks with my Pug in a dog park. How can I prevent other dogs from mauling her? A retractable leash will give her a bit of freedom and enable you to reel her in when another dog approaches. If an approaching dog is running free, prepare to lift your Pug and protect her until you have discovered the dog's intent. If the dog isn't aggressive, put your Pug on the ground. If untrustworthy, hold your Pug to your chest and walk away.

Chapter Three

How to Choose a Pug

I mpulse purchases are dangerous! Acquiring a lifelong companion is serious business that should be given considerable thought and preparation. Should you choose your companion on impulse, you will have many years to contemplate that mistake. Your Pug will no doubt be with you and will often remain in good health well into her teens. You must choose your companion from the best source and after considering your personal and family situations as well as all the idiosyncrasies of the breed.

A Pug is special. Your diminutive little pal will absorb a lot of your time. She needs frequent and thorough grooming. Training is a very important need that is also time-consuming. Muggs will require great amounts of playtime and human interaction, all of which are pleasant, but time-consuming duties. She needs gentle hands and a patiently compatible person who doesn't require immediate, perfect responses. When selecting your canine companion, look for personality, intelligence, talent, habits, and compatibility. Pugs are beautiful, but their physical attributes are less important than their more intangible features. If you keep that in mind when selecting your canine partner, you will enjoy many years of happiness.

Breed Needs

Muggs' greatest needs are your time and attention.

Are You Ready for a Pug?

Reliable facts are best acquired from people who own and take excellent care of their Pugs. To find such people, attend a local dog show, locate the Toy Group ring, and seek out the fanciers who hover around Pug crates. You probably are not seeking a show dog, but dog show people are the best-informed Pug fanciers you will find. Watch owner-handlers lovingly groom their proud charges, ask them questions, and praise their canine

companions. They will advise you of the benefits and downsides of owner-ship. They will explain about the time that must be allotted to Muggs every week, even if she is not kept in show condition.

You are the person who is ultimately responsible for purchase, but total agreement between all family members above the age of three or four years is critical. Toddlers will love whatever puppy you select and will be absolutely ecstatic if it is a clownish Pug. Pugs love children, especially small kids, with the taste of ice cream or cookies lingering on their cheeks or staining their bibs. If a child balks at having a dog of any kind, that's probably OK; the holdout will come around when the clown begins to show her stuff. Adolescent children and adults should agree on where Muggs sleeps, who is responsible for her feeding, who will take her for walks, and how many are willing to help with her grooming chores. Housebreaking and simple training is a breeze, but rules should be made and the trainer selected before the Pug is purchased. If your family is somewhat demo-cratic, discuss your puppy and take a vote.

CAUTION

Delegation of Duties

Don't delegate Muggs' care, feeding, and grooming to someone other than the adults of the family. Kids have a way of "forgetting" those activities in favor of computer games, ball practice, cheer-leading practice, dance lessons, and so forth. Be sure that at least one adult is in charge of Muggs' needs and sees to it that those duties are performed regularly and properly.

Choose the Right Time

The correct time of the year to purchase a Pug puppy is irrelevant, provided your house is not filled with family and friends. A Pug puppy needs peace and quiet for the first week or two. If possible, schedule Muggs' arrival to coincide with your vacation or at least a time when you will be home for a few days. Commotion and confusion interferes with housebreaking, sleeping adjustments, collar and leash training, introduction to and use of a toilet area in the yard, and Muggs' recognition of her name and family. A visiting neighbor child might accidentally step on or drop Muggs, but you will probably get the veterinary bill. Your free time should dictate the appropriate time to bring your new Pug into the house, and it should be when she is her family's center of attention.

So Many to Choose From

In 2007, there were 157 different AKC breeds in seven different groups to choose from. That doesn't include a few exotic breeds and others that are waiting in the wings to meet all the AKC registration criteria. Those numbers are mind boggling! Over 20 breeds are in the Toy Group. They are not just small terriers. How do you begin to choose a small-dog companion from that enormous array of candidates?

If you are considering a Pug and want the best one available, you may wait a long time before one is available in your area. Rescue Pugs are often available. If you are considering an adult companion, send your name to all the Pug rescue associations that are located within an accessible distance. Each rescue will ask you to keep in touch. The more times you call back, the better your chances will be.

For complete breed standards and pictures, buy or borrow from the library a current edition of the AKC's "The Complete Dog Book." Visit the AKC home page on the Internet. That reference will list the breed standard, history, place of origin, and each breed's function. A brief description of the general temperament or personality of each is also offered. If those data are carefully read and considered, you can decipher the high and low points of all AKC breeds that are currently available in the United States. The fallacy of trusting pictures or the usual written descriptions is that several breeds may have similar phenotypic (anatomic) characteristics. However, the temperament or personality of a puppy will vary according to the way she is chosen, handled, loved, housed, trained, and fed.

What Are Desirable Characteristics?

Are you seeking an animated mouse trap? Don't expect your Pug to possess that worthy talent because, unlike small terriers, the Pug wasn't developed to kill rodents. In fact, Muggs might ignore a mouse that happens by. At best, she might try to play with it. She doesn't have a killer instinct and really doesn't want to take on any new jobs. Muggs will very likely be momentarily fascinated by a little rodent, watch him for a while, and then stroll away.

Do you want a hunting or hiking buddy? Look elsewhere. Muggs is a great companion but one that prefers a short, leisurely walk on the lawn or sidewalk. She isn't into stalking the woods, firearms, sleeping bags, tents, and such. Muggs might retrieve a small, soft ball, but don't count on her to bring home your dinner entree. You expect her to pick up that bloody, feathered body? You must be kidding. You shot the pheasant, so you pick it up!

Is a shy, reserved little pet what you are looking for? One that sits on pillows and is more comfortable on your lap than on the floor? Do you want to shop for dog food that your pet will *consent* to eat? Muggs doesn't fit those descriptions either. As previously stated, a Pug will eat anything edible that hits the floor. This ambitious, outgoing companion will spend a limited amount of time on your lap. Most Pugs prefer floor action.

Consider what characteristics you want in the personal companion that will be under your feet and in need of training, grooming, and feeding next year and for the following 5, 10, or 15 years. List those characteristics before looking at pictures. Narrow the field by size, exercise requirements, coat type, personality, and behavior. Then select some breeds that you might consider. That task doesn't take much knowledge of the idiosyncrasies and personalities of breeds and is usually a decision based on pictures and personal preference.

- If you seek a small breed that stands no taller than 12 inches and weighs fewer than 20 pounds, you should check color pictures in one of several books devoted to small breeds or perhaps a dog encyclopedia.
- Exercise requirements are usually listed in those books as well. For instance, Jack Russell Terriers are cute but are wound up like springs, full of lively spirit, and demand a great amount of your time and effort. Some are more demanding than others, some are quieter or noisier than others, but all are full of fire and anxious to begin physical activity at the drop of a toy.
- Coat type is a factor that should never be forgotten because grooming often equates to personal time available. In America today, time is precious. Many small breeds possess beautifully colored, long coats that require regular and sometimes lengthy and complex grooming techniques to stay free of mats and tangles. Longhaired small dogs may be perfect for some owners, depending on the dogs' and owners' personalities.
- Consider personality, activity level, and behavioral traits. Are you looking for a hunting or hiking companion, or one that you can take on strolls and occasionally kick around a ball with? Are you seeking a stoic companion who rarely loses her composure? If so, the Pug is not your dog!

Breed Needs

Pug puppies, like all other pups, need their dam and siblings' socialization for a minimum of eight weeks.

Why a Pug?

All puppies are cute! Most are roly-poly, happy, and playful little balls of fur. If the puppies being considered are offered by reputable breeders, they will also be clean, active, and healthy. They will exhibit great curiosity, surround you, chew your shoestrings, and leap clumsily onto your legs. If you sit on the floor, they will wriggle all over, lick your face, perhaps woof excitedly, and appear to love you at first sight.

Of all toy breeds, the Pug is one favorite with increasing numbers of prospective owners. An adult Pug's attitude, personality, and temperament are a continuation of puppyhood. Once a clown, always a clown!

Best Age to Adopt a Pug Puppy

To become an excellent companion pet, a Pug puppy will benefit significantly from puppy play and dam-disciplined life for at least two months. Muggs will learn a great deal about pecking order and canine socialization while with siblings and will also benefit from human interaction and socialization through handling by the breeder's family.

Obtain reputable breeders' names from reliable sources. Never rely on photographs or seller's advice alone, and never acquire a puppy younger than eight weeks. Don't allow your emotions to choose a Pug puppy. Instead, consult the opinions of qualified advisors, including long-term owners, competent Pug breeders, and veterinarians.

Where to Purchase Your Puppy

Pet Pug buyers are in the majority and rightly so. Prospective Pug owners usually want a healthy, bright, and playful puppy that carries most of the Pug's physical and personality traits. They don't want their Pug to be shy, aggressive, or look like a mutt, but they are not ready to spend thousands of dollars for a nearly perfect Pug.

The American canine industry supports many and varied Pug vendors. Pet shops, backyard breeders, puppy mills, and newspaper advertisements are easily found. These must be evaluated carefully before you decide to make your purchase.

Pet Shops

Impulsive purchases are always risky. That applies doubly when purchasing a living animal to which you will commit your time and money for 15 years. Today's pet shops display a variety of frisky puppies in beautiful, spacious, and clean cubicles. Any playful puppy is difficult to resist, but you should be sure of the size, type, and breed of dog you seek. Check out a Pug's characteristics on the Internet or by attending a dog show. When you find one, check the temperament, conformation, color, and coat quality of the puppy before you buy. It is highly unlikely that you will be able to see a pet shop puppy's siblings or parents, but the shop owner may be able to furnish a pedigree or the breeder's name. If the puppy is AKC registered, you can usually trace its parentage through those records. If you find a Pug puppy that fits your needs and your budget in a pet shop, ask about the shop's policies and see proof of registration, health certification, vaccinations, related nutritional documents, and parasite control. Carefully read the shop's guarantee. Be sure you have return privileges with full refund if your veterinarian examines the puppy within 48 hours and finds it other than guaranteed.

Backyard Breeders

Amateur or backyard breeders are those individuals who own a female Pug, locate a male Pug owner in the neighborhood, and negotiate a mating between those two dogs. Many of these breeders usually have no knowledge of the Pug breed standard and lack experience with record-keeping, pedigrees, breeding techniques, and whelping procedures. Many backyard breeders have no idea what quality to expect from the puppies produced because often neither parent was checked for hereditary diseases. To many backyard litter owners, physical appearance and conformation are irrelevant as long as the puppy passes for a purebred Pug. Often the litter is not registered, because the people responsible for the breeding may not be familiar with AKC regulations. Sometimes a puppy is sold and accompanied by a copy of the dam's registration certificate. The buyer may not know the difference, and both buyer and seller are satisfied. Again, research the breeder you plan to buy from, and be sure all pups are up-to-date with their immunizations.

CAUTION

Backyard-bred puppies are usually peddled for a fraction of the cost of a reputable breeder's puppies, and buyers get exactly what they pay for.

When you buy a Pug, it is extremely important that you:

- Meet in person and converse with the person who bred your Pug.
- Visit the home in which your Pug was whelped and raised.
- Handle the puppy and its dam, siblings, and possibly other puppies or adults from the same bloodline.
- Be careful selecting which "expert" to believe—weed them out and never acquire your Pug puppy from a source in which breeding stock and pups are housed separately from the breeder's residence.

Puppy Mills

A puppy mill commonly keeps several bitches of several different breeds. They often own the sires of their litters as well. Most facilities are filthy, but a few have cleaned up their act and the kennels appear to be well-run. Their bitches are usually housed together, and you may find puppies of several litters in the same room with litters of other breeds. Management will display no ribbons or trophies. Almost always such an establishment is the cheapest place to buy a dog of any breed.

CAUTION

Puppy factories thrive on the outskirts of metropolitan areas where Pugs are popular.

Puppies bred at mills usually have poor conformation and questionable dispositions. They are born to pet-quality dams that look somewhat like other Pugs. Average pet-quality parents often produce pups that are afflicted with hereditary diseases. Human socialization is nearly always lacking in puppy mill pups. Those puppies develop undesirable habits and are difficult to housebreak and train.

Newspaper Advertisements

Ads are placed by backyard breeders, puppy mills, puppy thieves, and a few legitimate owners who must find new homes for their pets. A single Pug puppy that appears in an ad might be a windfall. If you call and then visit and handle the advertised Pug, you might acquire a great companion at a bargain price. Before you complete the deal, scan the owner's registration papers, guarantees, and information about the parents. Look at everything pertinent to the Pug that the present owner has. Then take the puppy to your veterinarian and, if possible, to a Pug breeder who can tell you more about the conformation of your possible acquisition. Maybe you'll be lucky!

Internet Advertisements

The names of conscientious and trustworthy Pug breeders and fanciers can be found on the Internet, but you need to know where to look and who to ask. Misinformed and irresponsible Pug fanciers may own web sites that are intermingled with legitimate ones.

In this digital era, scams appear in ads on the Internet. You should be wary of Internet information. Neither photographs nor sketchy descriptions of a Pug's quality can be trusted because the photo may not be that of the Pug whose name appears in the caption. Be very skeptical of chat lines and Internet-originated telephone conversations with Pug owners. Those people all have a product to sell. In the absence of personal contact, the information gleaned from those conversations should be considered hearsay and unreliable. Their advertisements may represent nothing more than puppy-mill operators or backyard breeders.

Competent Pug Breeders

Choose your Pug puppy from a home like your own but one in which a litter or two of beautiful Pug puppies are raised annually from the visible Pug bitches that were evaluated extensively and proven to be of breeding quality. The breeder who raises Pug puppies both scientifically and with love is the individual from whom you should buy.

Raising Pugs isn't a get-rich-quick business. It entails a great amount of knowledge and experience that can't be obtained solely from reading books. A reputable Pug breeder is a member of a local Pug club if one exists in his or

BE PREPARED! Questions to Ask the Breeder

1. How long have you been breeding Pugs?
2. How many litters do you raise each year?
3. Do you own the sire of this litter, and may I meet him?
4. Have the parents been proven clear for all possible hereditary diseases (eyes, hips, and so on)?
5. Do you routinely show your breeding stock, and have you any earned Champion of Record titles?
6. May I see a pedigree of this litter?
7. Has this litter been examined by your veterinarian?
8. Have they been vaccinated and if so, against which diseases?
9. Has the litter been checked for worms and if positive, when? Were they treated and with what medicine?
10. At what age will these puppies be ready to leave their dam?
11. What must I do to have my Pug puppy registered with the AKC?
12. How many times per day do I feed my puppy?
13. Will you furnish me with the name and some of the puppy's food?
14. Do you guarantee your Pug puppies?
15. May I leave a deposit with you and take the puppy to my veterinarian for examination?
16. Do you have a contract to cover this sale?

her area and is associated with a national or regional Pug Dog Club. He or she will guarantee the good health of all puppies that are sold and will begin human socialization of those puppies within the first few days of their lives.

To find a competent Pug breeder, attend a few dog shows and watch the Pugs parade. Most importantly, watch the owner-handlers of the Pugs who often are learned, expert breeders. Those hard-working people enjoy the companionship of Pugs and Pug owners. They come from all walks of life and share a common interest in their avocation, breeding and showing Pugs. They are serious about improving the breed through competitive shows judged under strict rules. Some breeder-handlers travel long distances on many weekends to exhibit their Pugs while hoping to earn another ribbon or trophy. When you meet an owner-breeder, strike up a conversation. You will be amazed at the information the person has at his or her fingertips and how willing the owner-breeder is to share that information. Collect business cards, make notes, and find out all you can about the person's Pug breeding operation.

If you are very lucky, you may find one or two reputable breeders who live nearby and have a litter of Pugs to sell. Make an appointment to visit the puppies and look at the facility in which they are raised. Pay special attention to the amount of interaction between the Pugs and their breeder's family.

Conscientious Pug breeders are honest, knowledgeable, reliable, and authoritative. They are proud to be professional dog people who have devoted their lives to

Breed Needs

All Pugs need human interaction from the day they are whelped onward in order to retain their instinctive, people-oriented attitudes and dispositions.

improving the Pug breed. Good breeders are those on whom you can depend for good advice in the future; they dote on their breeding stock and their avocation. That is important because few, if any, conscientious breeders are wealthy and powerful. Most, if not all, good breeders are involved as a sideline. Most have other sources of income that support their interest in Pugs.

You may be surprised at the number of questions that you will be asked when talking to a competent Pug breeder. The experience may make you

BE PREPARED! Questions the Breeder Will Ask You

1. Have you ever owned a toy breed before? If so, what breed?
2. How much spare time do you have per day to spend with your Pug?
3. Do you realize that a Pug is not a rugged outdoor dog?
4. Do you have the patience and sense of humor to deal with a clownish Pug?
5. Will you acquire the knowledge and take the time to train your Pug and teach her good manners?
6. Do you have a book on Pugs? Have you read it?
7. Do you have children, and if so, how old are they?
8. Do you live in a home with a fenced yard? If so, what type of fence is it?
9. Are you aware of the limitations on Pugs activities?
10. Are you aware of the grooming that is required for a Pug?
11. Will you invest in Pug accessories such as grooming gloves, nail clippers, and so forth?
12. Do you have a veterinarian, and if not, would you like a recommendation?
13. Will you have your puppy spayed (or neutered) at an early age?

If your meeting thus far has indicated that you are a responsible, loving, prospective owner, you may advance to the next stage of acquiring a Pug puppy.

- Ask to see any puppies the breeder has available.
- If he or she has no puppies at the present time, ask when a litter will be whelped. Try to negotiate your future purchase.
- Ask to see pet-quality pups, breeding stock, and retired show dogs.
- If a litter is available, you can expect the breeder to be very protective of them. Before allowing you to handle any of the Pugs, you will be asked if you have visited any other breeders' homes or pet shops prior to coming to the breeder's home. Your hands, clothing, and especially shoes can act as vectors or carriers for a number of transmissible diseases. If you answer yes, you may be asked not to touch any of the Pugs but may be allowed to view them from across the room.
- If you have not visited any other kennels today, the breeder will probably invite you to sit on the floor. You are in for the treat of your lifetime when he or she opens the door and you are deluged with Pug puppies, their mother, and possibly several more relatives. Your life will never be the same.

feel like you are adopting a human infant. The breeder will usually sell only after he or she is satisfied that you have sufficient knowledge to succeed in Pug ownership. The breeder may include addresses and phone numbers of Pug owners to contact and further your knowledge of Pug handling and training. The breeder will undoubtedly discuss your Pug's nutritional needs.

Choosing a Pug Puppy

Each Pug has his or her own personality and disposition. When you sit on the floor and let the litter swarm over your lap, you will have difficulty telling them apart. They are friendly, quick, mischievous little scamps that begin nibbling your shoelaces and end up licking your glasses. If you stand back a few feet and watch them as they work on your spouse's clothing, you might see that one is slightly less adventurous than another. One might show no fear of anything that moves. Another may be a little more apprehensive or display slower response time. Let the breeder help you decide on the best and most compatible choice for your family. He or she has gone through the puppy placement program many times and will strive to make you and your new Pug happy with your choice because, after all, that is your breeder's specialty!

Pet Puppy vs Show Dog

Reputable Pug breeders produce companion pets as well as fancy show dogs. Out of all Pug puppies born to AKC-champion parents, only a few are considered to be show prospects. The remainder are sold as pets. Pet Pugs are fine examples of the breed, and many will compare favorably with their show-dog-prospect siblings. Pet-quality Pug puppies sometimes lack proper balance of features, may be a smidgen too tall, or may not have the most desirable coat texture or color, but their parents passed all tests and examinations to prove they were hereditarily sound. They are pet-quality, beautiful, and with

41

CHECKLIST

Items to Have Upon Purchase

When you take Muggs home, she should be accompanied by several items:

✔ AKC puppy registration papers

✔ Record of her vaccinations, including name of the vaccine administered, diseases it is designed to protect against, and the dates of administration

✔ Record of fecal exams (for parasites), dates and results of the exams, treatments administered, and due date for future exams or treatments

✔ Pedigree (optional)

✔ Two-week's supply of Muggs' food and the specific feeding schedule that lists amounts and times of day for each meal

✔ Breeder's health guarantee

✔ Signed bill of sale

fine personalities, but they sell at a lower price than the nearer-perfect puppies. Non-show puppies are genetically just as healthy as their siblings.

Which Sex to Choose

Some prospective owners want a female Pug, others will settle only for a male. Gender is certainly your choice. If your Pug is bought as a companion and will be spayed or castrated, its sex is practically irrelevant. Males and females alike are expected to be fantastic companions.

Look Beyond the Health Guarantee

You are the buyer. At the time of purchase, you must accept or reject the seller's claim for the puppy's good health. Often Pug breeders guarantee the health of their puppies, but never take that guarantee beyond its literal meaning. Take your puppy to your veterinarian immediately upon leaving the breeder, not tomorrow or a week from today.

Ask the breeder to accompany you or to hold your partial payment. Many veterinarians will perform a pre-purchase examination free of charge. If you must pay for the exam, do so. If the veterinarian is satisfied with the Pug's present health and you are satisfied with your interview with the breeder and with your choice, you are ready to finalize your purchase. A guarantee may specify that if you are unable to keep Muggs, the breeder will take her back, with or without refund. The contract may assign limitations on time and amount of cash rebate that are agreed upon by both

parties. It may state that if Muggs is diagnosed with a hereditary problem in the future, the breeder will furnish a replacement puppy at little or no cost. Ask to see proof of the dam's and sire's genetic eye health and physical soundness. If the litter has been seen by a veterinarian, ask to see the results of the exam, vaccinations administered, and de-worming treatments and recommendations. A guarantee isn't worth the paper it is written on unless it is dated and signed by the breeder. Never purchase a puppy unless you can take it to your veterinarian directly from the breeder's home.

Good Health Is Essential

Sound health is probably the most important factor in your quest for a great Pug puppy. Without excellent health, you are wasting your money on a cute puppy. Remember that all Pug pups are cute, regardless of their state of health. After you have evaluated the home of the breeder and met the adult Pugs of the family, look at the litter from a distance (if that is possible). All puppies five to eight weeks old should be playing, sleeping, or eating. If one looks different from the others, it might be timid or ill. You should note that. Timid Pugs usually aren't found. When they are, they may not make acceptable companion pets. An ill Pug should never be considered.

DNA and Canine Health Information Center (CHIC)

Most canine fanciers of all breeds are aware of DNA tests that are commonly taken to prove or disprove parentage or genetic relationship of dogs to one another. An in-depth discussion of genetics is beyond the scope of this book, but an introduction to that fascinating science is appropriate. Until recently, selective breeding was used to eliminate a hereditary disease from a bloodline. For a number of reasons, the effort to eradicate those genetically transmitted conditions from a breed is not totally effective. The CHIC plan assumes that if a puppy develops a genetically transmitted condition, one or both of its parents will be excluded from the breed's future gene pool and other dogs of the same bloodline are under suspicion. The plan then researches pedigrees and health records for signs of hereditary diseases throughout the breed. Actions are begun to stop future breeding that may promote or allow the defect. That plan is only as effective as the honesty of the dog owner participants.

The combination of individual dog identities, pedigrees, health histories, and DNA tissue or blood sample analyses are now being sought that, when scientifically compared, may identify hereditary disease risks in the breed. The result of CHIC DNA testing will eventually improve the ability of novice dog owners, like you, to find the best Pug available. The hope is that the testing will ultimately reduce and perhaps eliminate hereditary canine diseases.

Pug Rescue

Pug puppies are cute, but older Pugs are just as cute and they come without housebreaking chores and leash training. If you are looking for an adult Pug and are not afraid of taking a modest risk, investigate the adoption of a rescued Pug. Although they aren't numerous, stray or unwanted Pugs sometimes end up in rescue organizations. If you adopt a rescued adult and find that you are unable to keep her, that organization should agree to take her back. A rescued Pug is nearly always kept in a foster home until her health and personality are evaluated by experienced owners that are also Pug breeders. A rescued Pug is routinely neutered, vaccinated, implanted with an identification microchip, and in good health. She carries a modest price, and the money is used to support the work of the voluntary rescue organization.

Breed Truths

A rescue Pug may continue to watch for a well-loved buddy to arrive, but she won't pine over his absence.

From personal experience, a rescued Pug is wholeheartedly recommended! It is true that an older dog requires a longer bonding experience before she is totally comfortable in her new home. A Pug never forgets the voices, faces, and actions of her first owners. However, a Pug is so malleable and people oriented that she will be able to overcome the grief resulting from the loss of her previous family and accept your home and family within a few days.

If you want to adopt an older Pug, contact the Pug Dog Club of America and ask about Pug rescue organizations. Next, contact Pug breeders in your area and let them know you are in the market for an adult Pug. While waiting for a response, go to nearby shelters and put up a sign with your name and phone number offering to give a good home to an adult Pug. You might get lucky and find one right away, or you might wait a year. However, success will make your wait worthwhile.

Pug Rescue Organizations

At least a dozen rescues can be found by typing "Pug rescue organizations" on your computer's Internet search line. Some sites are general and some are state oriented, but most will help you find an adult Pug. Some rescued Pugs have undergone personality, canine etiquette, and manners evaluations by behavioral experts, but that is probably overkill in the case of a Pug. Adult Pugs usually retain their senses of humor and will remain clownish the rest of their lives.

Chapter Four

Caring for a Pug Puppy

Y ou will probably have a few days between the time you arrange for Muggs' purchase and the time you actually bring her home. Use that time productively. Don't forget that many pet supply stores, variety stores, and thrift shops are available where you can find what she needs. (The prices of items shown in the text were the averages found in local pet supply stores as of May 2008.)

Lifestyle Changes

Puppies always upset established routines. When you decide upon a new addition to your family, you should review the changes, such as recreation, that will take place in your habits. You've decided to yield a certain amount of television viewing in favor of spending time with your little companion, but that isn't as terrible as it sounds. For

Helpful Hints

Take the time to shop around and locate the appropriate items, always considering quality as well as price.

instance, training and grooming Muggs will absorb significant time. However, an easy way to attack that duty is to space the 15-minute sessions in the early mornings and evenings. Playing with her will be so much fun that it can be done most any time and will soon be the highlight of your day.

Soon after acquiring Muggs, you will begin to ask yourself a question, "Who is this little Cleopatra?" She will claim top billing, and your family will be eating from her paw within a few weeks. You will shop for new toys for her to carry around. You may discover that previously unknown training talents become more viable with such a clever student. Some unsophisticated Pug owners are occasionally caught sitting on the floor playing with their Pugs. You may be tempted to take Muggs for a quick trip to the park and miss your favorite TV program. Petting and grooming will become more important and more enjoyable than you believed possible. You might even start talking to Muggs as if she knew exactly what you were saying.

Helpful Hints

Have Food Ready Before Muggs Arrives

Use the breeder's puppy food that he or she sent with Muggs, and don't change your Pug's diet for at least a week. If you decide to change her diet, change it a little at a time, and follow the directions on page 135. Wash Muggs' food and water dishes in the dishwasher, or scrub them in the sink each day. Keep a supply of fresh drinking water for her all day until about an hour before retiring for the night. Under normal circumstances, she doesn't need access to water at night.

You may unwind, sit down, relax, and enjoy your life.

Remember the term of commitment; your Pug puppy will probably live for 15 years. Don't forget that you need a healthy sense of humor, abundant patience, and plenty of time to enjoy your puppy's play time, home examinations, grooming, and training. Prepare and acquire the knowledge to tackle Muggs' socialization with other dogs and humans. Your budget must provide the funds for your Pug's needs, which include the initial and continuing cost of annual exams and vaccinations, dog food, parasite control, and other necessities. If you travel and Muggs can't go with you, it is important to remember to make arrangements to board her with a friend or relative.

Sleeping Arrangements

Muggs should be given a safe, warm, cuddly place to spend the night that is in close proximity to where you sleep. That's not to suggest that Muggs share a bed with a family member, because that behavior can cause many problems. A fiberglass crate in your bedroom makes an ideal Pug den. In a well-bedded crate, she is safe from dangers. You can also hear her nighttime restlessness and take her out. Furnishing such a haven averts several accident risks. When a pup is loose in the house, she may fall down stairs or be tripped over in the dark by a sleepy child. A crate will also enhance housebreaking (see page 74).

Puppy-proofing Your Life

Never leave Muggs alone in an unprotected room. Put up your X-pen. Use it each time you leave her sight, especially when you are cooking or eating meals and when guests come to play cards.

However, a pen can be overused, and that is equivalent to puppy abuse. Muggs needs to follow you around, chewing your shoelaces, tugging your pants leg, and generally getting under your feet. That's what puppies are all about.

Pug puppies are people oriented, and they want to be with you whether or not it is convenient for you. Learn to walk with a shuffle to prevent stepping on little feet. Watch your step to preclude kicking or stepping on

SHOPPING LIST

Pug Necessities

✔ Bed of some type. It can be a folded blanket or a foam bed that is big enough for an adult Pug. ($20 new, $5–$10 in thrift store) A wicker bed is not recommended because puppies may chew it.

✔ Fiberglass crate or kennel that is large enough for an adult Pug to stand and turn around in comfortably. ($20–$30 new, $5–$10 in thrift store)

✔ Folding X-pen or movable wire mesh pen, about 16 feet in circumference. ($70 new, $15 in thrift stores)

✔ Lightweight, soft nylon web harness. ($8–$10 new)

✔ Lightweight nylon leash about 4 or five 5 long. ($6–$8 new)

✔ Lightweight, strong, braided nylon cord about 25 feet long. ($4 at hardware stores)

✔ Four stainless steel dishes. Buy two in a metal rack that raises them about 4 inches above the floor and two alternate dishes without the rack. Plastic dishes aren't good because chemicals used in manufacturing will leach into water or damp food. Ceramic bowls are no good because glazing chemicals can contaminate water. Glass dishes break and last only about a week. ($20 new for rack and 2 dishes)

✔ Pug-tight backyard fence, wooden, block, or chain-link.

✔ Name tag with your name, address, and phone number. The tag should be riveted to her harness. ($2)

✔ Grooming supplies (See Chapter 7).

✔ Dental equipment, such as a finger brush ($5 for two) or a canine toothbrush ($3.50) and some canine toothpaste ($2.50). Do not use people, mint-flavored toothpaste.

✔ Training treats, either homemade or commercial, low-calorie tidbits. ($2–$4)

✔ Nylon bones or twisted rawhide sticks that are formed from ground-up rawhide. It may be risky to allow Muggs to chew one-piece rawhide. Some authorities claim that one-piece rawhide sticks can be risky if they are swallowed. Discard half-eaten rawhide sticks to prevent them being caught in her throat or being swallowed and requiring surgical removal. ($2–$4 per bag)

✔ Small stuffed dog or cat toys ($2.50–$5) that you can use when playing with Muggs. Remember that she and stuffed toys should never be left alone together until her chewing stage has ceased.

Muggs, who is rarely out of your field of vision. She doesn't seek out ways to hurt herself, but your job is to see that hazards are removed before she arrives. She isn't an uncontrollable chewer, but she can acquire that habit if you allow her to chew whatever she picks up. Her chewing usually destroys only the object being chewed. Sometimes she will chew off pieces. If swallowed, they may cause intestinal damage.

Don't allow an uninstructed child to pick up and carry Muggs. Pug puppies are tough little critters, but their bones break. Fractures hurt a lot and are very expensive to repair.

Pug-proofing the Backyard

Dogs learn about their environment by tasting anything they see. That can be a serious or even fatal mistake for Muggs

CAUTION

Never lift Muggs to a bed, chair, or any other elevated place. She is sure to fall or jump the second you turn your back.

to make. Hidden hazards lurk behind every bush and around every corner. A sack of powdered insecticide might have a teaspoonful of poison spilled on the outside, just waiting to be licked up by an unsuspecting Muggs. An herbicide bottle with some dried plant poison on its side might be lying around, or the yard fence might have a tiny hole in it, just big enough for little Muggs to squeeze through. Once out of her yard, Muggs is a stray. She may be quite sociable, but the big, aggressive dog down the street might not wait for a formal introduction. Neighborhood kids with air rifles may try to discipline the wandering Pug, or worse, Muggs may meet with a moving car.

HOME BASICS
Home Hazards

Guard against the following hazards.

- Stairs are especially dangerous until she learns how to walk up and down them and should be protected with gates that are specially made for that purpose. ($30 in pet supply store)
- Electric and electronic cords hanging within reach of Muggs' teeth.
- Edible items that are left within her reach, such as cat food, which is much too rich for her.
- Cat boxes that naturally contain both litter and feline fecal matter. A Pug will snack on cat feces, so buy your cat a "Buda Box" that has a door.
- Artificial or natural houseplants, especially those that hang lower than the tabletop.
- Infant and toddlers' teething rings, pacifiers, wooden or plastic blocks, and stuffed toys.
- Pencils, pens, paper clips, and waste baskets that are fair game for an inquisitive Pug puppy.
- Pillow fringes that hang within Muggs' reach.
- Cupboard doors should be closed. Many kitchen chemicals are toxic.
- Table crumbs should be picked up instantly.
- Lower-shelf books, especially expensive first editions.

Pick up any miscellaneous rubbish and decaying vegetation that have been piled behind the garden shed, because it can be a dangerous attraction for your little companion. Be sure garden chemicals are stored well out of Muggs' reach and sprayers and spreaders are hung at a safe elevation.

Those seemingly obvious threats to Muggs' life, plus many more, can present themselves at any time. Be alert to those dangers that have not seemed important before Muggs but now are critical to your companion's health.

Swimming Pool If a pool is part of your backyard landscape and the fence is not Pug-proof, the pool should be equipped with an exit ramp for Muggs to use should she fall in. Hold a pool drill to teach Muggs where and how to get out of the pool.

Invisible Fences A recent rage in dogdom is an invisible, electronic fence consisting of a transmitting wire that is buried a few inches deep around the perimeter of your yard. Your Pug wears a collar that is equipped with a receiver. When she approaches the underground wire, the collar emits a warning sound. If she ventures closer to the buried wire, a shock is transmitted from the wire and received by the dog.

Invisible fences have at least one major shortcoming. They allow other dogs and wild animals into your yard. A big, aggressive dog can wander over the buried wire at will and put Muggs' life at risk.

Wire Fence Some fences are made of chain-link fabric with the posts set in concrete. The lawn is soft and cool; the yard provides sunshine, shade, and a place for Muggs to exercise to her heart's content. Make sure the wires and gate posts are fastened tightly together. Boredom is the primary cause of escape from a yard. Boredom will stimulate digging, climbing, or squeezing through any tiny space. Pugs are clever creatures and will find a way to get to children or other attractive nuisances if they're left alone for extended periods.

All-day backyard living for your Pug is a mistake. If you have a secure yard, she may be safe. However, Muggs is like any other family member and wants to live with the family, in and out of the house. The yard is a wonderful place to play, to train, and to exercise, but she needs to be with her family.

Automobiles and Big Dogs

You may think that Muggs is smart enough to stay out of the street, but don't count on it.

One of the most likely reasons for Muggs to occupy an emergency table is being hit by a car. A 14-pound Pug always comes out second best in a collision with a 2,000-pound vehicle. The result is often death or serious injuries, which may include shock, fractures, hemorrhage, and other disabling and possibly incurable conditions. For those reasons, you should always keep her restrained and safe with harness and leash when venturing outside her backyard.

Always be mindful of Muggs' size. She is less than a foot tall and doesn't present an object that is easily seen by drivers. She is virtually invisible to a driver when she darts from your presence into a street. She's especially vulnerable because of her sociable nature and habit of joining children at play. She spots a game across the street, decides to join in, and darts away. A dog twice her size may instead chase her into the path of a vehicle. Be sure all fences are secure and there is no chance Muggs can escape from your backyard and into the pathway of a moving car.

Wooden Fence If the fence is constructed from slats, be certain that every slat touches the ground, leaving no space for your Pug to duck under. If Muggs has the time and opportunity to wriggle through, she will join kids at play on the other side.

Garage Dangers

Garages nearly always contain chemicals. If you don't have cupboards with latches on doors, chemicals such as paint thinner, gasoline, and windshield washer fluid should be put out of Muggs' reach. Dogs are known to lick up

oil, regardless of its foul taste, and sweet-flavored antifreeze may be the most toxic fluid found in your garage.

Bonding

Bonding is the process of establishing a trusting relationship between human and Pug. A bond is a complex alliance, a uniting force, the developing of a mutually binding covenant. You can't hurry bonding. It means talking to your Pug all the time she is with you. Muggs won't understand what you mean if you mention bonding. However, talking to her shows you are interested in her and will increase the bond between you. Mutual trust, love, obedience, and confidence are intangible parts of the bonding process.

CAUTION

Raisins and grapes are claimed to be causes of acute kidney failure in dogs. Don't use them as training rewards or leave them within reach of your pug.

Puppy Bonding

Bonding continues throughout Muggs' life. However, the prime time for it is when she is very young and inexperienced. She is intelligent and adventuresome, but her prior knowledge is limited to her breeder's handling before weaning. She knows very little about human involvement and lifestyles. Breeders' families wisely handle

HOME BASICS
Appreciation of Your Pug

- Grooming Muggs frequently will increase your appreciation of her.
- Muggs is entitled to *always* be handled with gentleness and love.
- Training and games are excellent challenges for your Pug's mind.
- The only appropriate response to Muggs' errors is correction, never punishment.

- A significant health consideration is guarding against obesity.
- Try to match your sense of humor with that of Muggs.
- Be considerate about Muggs' sensitivity to heat and excessive activity.

all puppies while they are still in the nest, but that is not nearly as important as the contact she receives after leaving it.

You removed her from all the security and limitations of the only home she has ever known. Muggs is a frightened, helpless little Pug and must be terrified by her prospects. The first thing she realizes when she is thrust into the strange new environment is that her mother and siblings are gone. You must insert yourself and your family into that void, providing companionship, love, and care. Hold her, pet her, feed her, groom her, and make her comfortable. If she cries for her mother and siblings, console her.

Her response is to appreciate and love you. More than that, she learns to focus on you and depend on you. While you are gently caring for her as a matter of duty, she's bonding with you more tightly. Soon, she will look to you not only for food and comfort but also for play, exercise, and virtually every enjoyable activity. You call her name in a certain soft tone, and she responds by coming to you as naturally as if she was always yours and was always named Muggs. You reward her response with kind words and petting to show that she is responding properly. Bonding goes on throughout life, and the relationship between Pug and owner continues to build forever.

Adult Bonding
If you adopt a grown Pug instead of a puppy, she will become part of your family. However, she must be made welcome in your home. Bonding is extremely important with adult Pugs. If another family has raised

FYI: What's in a Name?

If you don't know your adult Pug's name, you must assign one. Choose a simple, one- or two-syllable word that fits her looks or personality. Changing Muggs' name has no value if she came from a loving home with no negative experiences. To minimize the stresses of change, continue using her former name. If you adopt an abandoned Pug and her former name is unknown or isn't agreeable with you, give her a new name right away. Pick a one- or two-syllable word that fits her description or personality, and use it often. She will eventually respond to it.

Yelling her name is a waste of time. Muggs' hearing is superior to yours, and a conversational tone is sufficient. Call her frequently by saying in a normal voice, "Muggs, come," and reward her arrival with a tasty tidbit. Make the food treat something special, something she likes. That's easy with a Pug, because you will rarely find a food that Muggs doesn't like. Pet and praise her for responding to your call. If she is slow to respond, don't despair. Keep a pocketful of tasty treats.

Muggs and you obtained her from a pound or foster home, you may have a minimal idea about how she was handled previously, or you may not have a clue. Bonding moves slower between adult dogs and new owners, but the basics are the same.

Patience is necessary. It is critically important not to rush the bonding process. Be available to Muggs, but don't force the issue. Always encourage her, but allow her to come to you. Muggs will become accustomed to her new home and family in her own time, which may be a matter of days, weeks, or months. Don't give up. If she hasn't bonded with you in a reasonable time, consult with the person who was fostering her.

If Muggs was a stray and her past is unknown, allow her to move about your home and yard without harness or leash for a few days. When she accepts the harness, try snapping on a leash to see what happens. If she has been taken for walks in the past, she will indicate her acceptance of the leash quickly and anxiously.

Experiment with various games, activities, and toys to discover which ones your adult Pug knows and likes best. After you've discovered a few of the activities she enjoys, ask her to play those games or perform those tasks. If she responds to a particular toy or game such as fetching, toss a knotted piece of cotton rope. When she brings it straight to you, tell her, "Muggs, give," and offer her a treat. She can't accept the treat without dropping the rope. She will thus learn to focus on you and respond to you. Your actions won't strain your relationship.

Don't put Muggs into an untenable situation. Try to make her believe that everything she does is correct. Ignore her lack of appropriate response to a command, and concentrate on tasks she does willingly and well. Above

all, talk to Muggs. Second only to food, your gentle voice and touch are the most important tools to use when bonding with a grown Pug. If she consistently hears you speaking her new name and your verbal assurances, she will soon respond and seek your attention, the treat, and your verbal approval.

Grown dogs must always be handled carefully, but that's doubly true when you have children. Unless your kids are old enough to understand the situation, it probably is best not to introduce Muggs to toddlers right away. Although unreliable or ornery Pugs are rare, be sure the new Pug is trustworthy. Let her acclimate to you and your home first, before moving ahead with family introductions.

Handling Your Pug Puppy

Your Pug puppy has a built-in trust in her human family, but you must enhance that credibility. Muggs is tiny, about six inches tall, and you are an adult, perhaps five or six feet tall. She may remember being lifted

Helpful Hints

Teaching Muggs Her Name and *Come*

Muggs has a great appetite, so make use of it. Call her name frequently. When she responds, reward her for coming. During the first few months, her rewards should be verbal praise, petting, and a tiny savory treat. Food treats are highly effective, even when they are quite small.

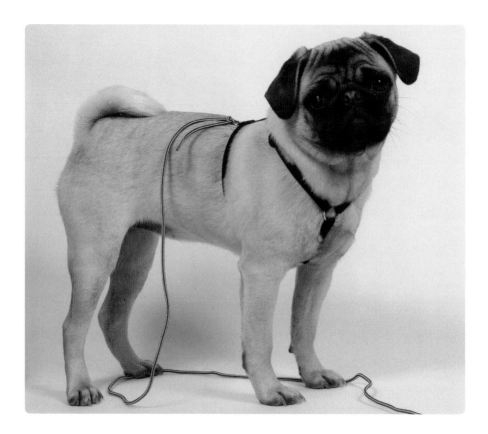

into or out of her nest, but she has no experience even vaguely similar to being lifted high above the floor. She quivers and shakes when you begin. Take care not to frighten her, and be reassuring. Never hurry, and always talk softly. If you try using one hand to lift her, she will be afraid of falling, stiffen up, and wriggle. You may drop her. One fall will cause panic, lack of trust, and possible injury. In the future, she may refuse to come when you call, her confidence in you will suffer, and you certainly will spoil an otherwise positive training experience.

Instead, kneel down or sit on the floor, and let her climb on your lap. Slide one hand under her chest and abdomen. Place your other hand over her spine, using firmness but without squeezing. Then, while holding her firmly against your chest, rise in a slow and deliberate manner. Walk a few steps, kneel down, and place her gently back on the floor, making sure all four feet are safely down before releasing her. Give her a treat immediately after she reaches the floor to bolster her confidence in you. After a few such trials, her trust will build, and each time will be easier for her to cope. All pre-teen children should be instructed to sit or lie down on the floor, let Muggs climb all over them or on their laps, but absolutely do not lift her. Hold a training session for your adolescent children to teach them the proper method of lifting and carrying their little buddy.

Collar or Harness?

A Pug usually doesn't like to wear a collar unless it is absolutely necessary. Muggs' head is rather large. Any collar can be quite uncomfortable when it slides up behind her ears, even though nylon web collars are softer than leather ones. A harness is much more suitable for her, except if she is entered in a dog show, wherein a judge can require every dog to wear a collar when being exhibited in the show ring. If that time comes, Muggs can wear a slip-collar that is attached to the leash

Full-time harness wearing is a judgment call. Her identification tag should be riveted on her harness, and she should be walked outside the yard only when on lead and safely under your protection. When both of you are in the house or if she is running around her backyard and you are positive that your yard is Pug-tight, you can leave the harness hanging in a handy place.

Identification

The name tag you buy for Muggs should be riveted tightly to her harness and not fastened by an S-hook, which can hang up on tree or bush. Until you buy a tag, a waterproof marking pen can be used to print your name, address, and phone number on her harness. Pugs may be stolen and sold to Pug fanciers in another town, or they may be peddled in other markets. If you desire a more permanent identification, two types are available.

A microchip carries extensive, permanent identification and can be painlessly implanted under Muggs' skin (without general anesthesia) by a veterinarian, at a cost of about $90. Some breeders have chips implanted before the pups are placed in new homes. Occasionally dog clubs furnish chip implantation at greatly discounted prices. Microchips are easily read by an electronic device similar to a bar code reader.

Tattooing is the other permanent identification. If possible, it should be done when Muggs is under anesthesia for another procedure, such as spaying or castration. Tattoos are used with great success in identifying and proving ownership of dogs. Prices vary, so check with your veterinarian or your local Pug club regarding tattooing.

Human Socialization

Human socialization is inborn in a Pug. Muggs wants to please people, and she rarely fails to do so. You might need to polish up her rough edges. However, she likes living in a human environment and acts like she is a full-fledged family member. She is a happy little companion and is compatible with nearly everyone she meets. Her favorite pastime is playing games with the kids and entertaining her family with her clownish antics. Sometimes she will chase her playmates, either humans or pets. Sometimes she will run from them, encouraging a quick game of tag. Muggs is a people pleaser. Everyone wants to pet and play with her, and she wants to reciprocate. Her greatest fear is being left out of a family gathering. It is easy to include a Pug factor in every function your family plans, but don't expect her to take a back seat to anyone, whether two or four legged.

Helpful Hints

Many animal shelters now implant microchips in every adopted dog, and those agencies may provide that service or tattooing for a greatly reduced fee.

Rarely will a Pug be afraid or shy around strange people. Socialization with friends and neighbors comes naturally to Muggs. From puppyhood to maturity, she is ready to meet anyone anywhere. She greets strangers with a smile and generally makes a nuisance of herself during their visits to your home. If she shows any timidity or shyness, or if she leaves the room when they arrive, tell them to ignore Muggs. Ask your guests to occasionally give Muggs a treat that you provide when they arrive. Sooner or later, she will show interest. At that time, the guests can offer her a tiny tidbit. Muggs will enjoy your friends' generosity. Next time, they will be greeted as old friends, with a smile and wriggle.

BREED COMPATIBILITY

Pugs are naturally nonaggressive and typically are compatible with nonaggressive breeds of all sizes. However, to be safe, allow her to play and exercise off-lead with dogs of her own size, which include:

- Affenpinscher
- Brussels Griffon
- Chihuahua
- English Toy Spaniel
- Italian Greyhound
- Japanese Chin
- Maltese
- Toy Manchester Terrier

- Miniature Pinscher
- Papillon
- Pekingese
- Pomeranian
- Toy Poodle
- Shih Tzu
- Silky Terrier
- Yorkshire Terrier

Canine Socialization

Muggs was probably socialized with other puppies in her litter and possibly with other canine pets before you acquired her, but those events shouldn't be taken for granted. Often a new Pug puppy lacks the social graces needed to mingle with other dogs, most of whom are larger than she is.

After receiving the appropriate immunizations, encourage Muggs to play with other puppies of the same general size and age. Walk her on leash in the park or your neighborhood. Allow her to sniff and bounce around in the presence of her peers while you hold her leash. Usually she will be safe in a supervised, unleashed, canine social circle, such as a kindergarten class where small breed pups play and wrestle harmlessly with others of their size. A Pug usually will choose another Pug-size pup when wrestling teams are selected, but those classes should be monitored closely.

CAUTION

Closely monitor any situation when Muggs is in the presence of strange dogs. She could be bitten badly if she happens upon an uncontrolled dog on a walk, and you should be prepared to protect her from those encounters.

Pugs aren't troublemakers. They usually will not start a fight, nor will they participate in any scraps that erupt between other dogs. Muggs is a strong, little dog who doesn't have a pugnacious nature. You will usually find her observing from a safe distance when an altercation occurs. She will appreciate being lifted and carried whenever larger, aggressive dogs are met. Dogs of her own size may stalk each other, walk on stiff legs, and raise their hackles, but most are showoffs that actually mean no harm.

Communicating with Your Pug

Voice Pugs are quite capable of perceiving the slightest change in your voice. Modulation of your voice will tell Muggs whether she is being complimented or criticized. Shouting is a waste of time. Her auditory sense is better than yours, and a slight change in voice timbre is sufficient to tell her that you are speaking to her. Muggs will remember that one word in your conversation with a guest that may turn on her action switch and produce a performance that wasn't meant to happen, at least not at that time. Her forlorn expression and turning of her head from side to side while you are speaking to her doesn't necessarily mean that she understands your conversation. It may indicate that she is listening for a familiar word, a key to what you expect of her, or a sign that it is her turn to respond. Praise will reinforce her focus on you, and a tasty reward will tell her that you approve of her actions.

Hands Hand signals should accompany teaching Muggs fun commands, such as *dance*, *up*, *roll*, or *bang*, but those manual signs are rarely necessary after the initial training sessions. Other hand signals can be essential means of communication in obedience work. Those silent signals include *down*, *stay*, *over*, and *come*. In obedience work, Muggs can be taught *recall* when you wave to her, *stop* when she sees your hand extended in a flat, fingers up position, and turn *right* or *left* when the fingers of your hand are extended in those directions. She can be taught to follow your pointing when she is playing "hide the treat." Like any other training, silent hand signals should be taught with praise and reward for satisfactory response, and errors should be ignored with silence.

Facial Expressions A Pug's clown-like, wrinkled face can ask questions and express pleasure or remorse quite plainly. Never scold a child in her presence, or your Pug's eyes may immediately take on a sad appearance. Her facial features will sag and ears will drop, and she will turn and slowly walk away. Is her response because she thinks you are scolding her, or is it in sympathy for her playmate? Muggs is an expert at changing her expression in response to your voice, even when you are not directing your words to her. She may frown when she doesn't understand what you are saying, as if to signal you to slow down and repeat. That expression may also be seen while you are speaking to a guest or another family member. Is she actually *reasoning* when she dons that quizzical mask, or is she simply waiting for the next recognizable signal from you?

Body Movement

Pugs wag when they are happy or seeking your approval. They drop their heads and cease wagging when they are unhappy, unwell, or afraid. Most other dogs' standing neck hair, stiff legged gaits, growls, and snarls are signs that they are in a fighting mood, and turning belly up is a signal to the opponent that the dog concedes defeat in the fight. However, Muggs is a lover not a fighter. It is doubtful if you will ever hear Muggs growl or see her snarl. She may pull her lips back in a happy grin, but that is a transitory expression that has no sinister meaning. She drops and turns belly up to signal that she wants a belly rub. Personal body language should be carefully gauged to take on similar, positive meanings. You should never make threatening movements toward your Pug, even in play. Never lose your temper and sense of humor, or her personality will never develop into the happy, loving, amusing little clown you want her to be.

Scents

Pugs have significant scenting ability, but they haven't become working dogs such as retrievers, avalanche dogs, or drug scenting dogs. Muggs can usually find a treat hidden under a rug. When she is on a walk, she will stop, sniff, and mark where other dogs have urinated. However, she has only a passive interest in where each quail or dove has settled in the grass or the direction a bunny took when it crossed her path a few seconds ago. Some dogs are believed to recognize the scent of serious human diseases. Muggs, in the role of a therapy dog, changes her expression when she enters a hospice. Is that because she scents an illness, or do the physical surroundings and sick-room smells stimulate her sympathy? Pheromones are possibly scent oriented. Does Muggs read those pheromones that we exude when we are afraid or injured, or does her well-tuned focus on her companions' emotions tell her to sympathize? We may never know the answers, but we can be sure that our Pug sincerely matches our moods and gives us support in times of need.

Chapter Five

Living with and Training a Pug

Muggs is a companion and a friend. She is a dog, but she's special and smart! Despite her cuteness, her size, and her clownishness, she is, after all, a dog. Cute can be a handicap because cuteness wears off with time. If a reasonable amount of training hasn't taken place during that period, you and Muggs are in big trouble. Smart is OK. Be careful, though, because a clever dog has been known to outwit an unsuspecting owner. Neither cute nor clever can be substituted for good manners, obedience, or an obliging attitude. No matter how personal your relationship, your four-legged companion is your possession by law and a canine by birth. It's true that you share your home and perhaps your bed with her, take her on walks, and groom and talk to her. You share your time with her, care for her, and clean up after her. Still, she is a dog. Muggs is a personable little gal that often does not act doggish. She is a clown, a constant source of joy to you. However, you don't need DNA evidence to prove that your Pug is a *Canis familiaris*, a domestic dog!

Helpful Hints

Muggs prefers to be left on the floor and not carried about, even by her adult owners.

Pugs and Children

Your companion is a solidly built and sturdy little dog that is the largest member of the AKC Toy Group. However, she won't thrive on kids' rough and tumble, tug-of-war games. Leave those sports to the Labs and Golden Retrievers.

Pugs identify with and appreciate small children, possibly because those toddlers are clownish too. More likely, Muggs just likes to lick the youngsters' jelly-flavored faces. She is a wonderful playmate and loves hide-and-seek games. Many Pugs will fetch, but don't expect the ball to be promptly returned to you after she picks it up. Adolescent children often bond strongly with the family Pug. She appreciates them petting her and sitting on their laps as well as accompanying the youths on short, leashed jaunts around the neighborhood.

Parents use words like playful, lively, and unreservedly responsive when describing their Pug's devotion to children of the family. Muggs will never be aloof or indifferent to a play session. Only when fatigue approaches will she retire to her crate or bed for a nap. She is ready for any activity and is a dedicated participant in children's games, barring an accidental fall or being stepped on by a careless playmate.

Pugs and Other Pets

Your Pug would prefer to be an only child, the one who always captures the spotlight. Muggs will naturally prefer to be the sole house pet to assure that she is the center of attention. Other Pugs in the home are accepted quickly. They may form an alliance, cohabit peacefully, play together, and invent games and other diversions to entertain human residents.

Cats and small dogs are usually quite safe with a well-socialized Pug. In the event new pets are acquired, introductions should be carefully managed. For instance, if a new housecat has its claws intact, it's best to trim them to protect Muggs' eyes if kitty should take offense at being licked, pawed, or otherwise pestered.

Large dogs are usually ignored by your Pug, but a big dog may be bothered by Muggs' inherent audacity. It is highly unlikely that she will vie for supremacy in the canine pecking order, but she is not mentally or physically equipped to defend herself against a larger housemate's attacks. If you are inclined to keep a large dog in the home with her, always be on your guard. Alpha dog contests are usually won by the aggressor—the one with the sharp teeth and impatient attitude. That is true even if the crafty Pug admits defeat before the contest begins.

Training Basics

You might hear the remark, "Muggs is smart!" Actually, she may possess below-average intelligence but has been well trained and displays a burning desire to please her owner. She excitedly yearns for the chance to display her canine experience and ability. Being clever is a start, but training is the key to owning a great companion dog!

It will soon be apparent that this chapter contains no radical training techniques, nothing magical, mysterious, new, or earth shattering. Instead, a logical progression from one point to the next is offered with some important facts for you to remember. Schooling can be discussed in a step-by-step manner, but in application, it rarely takes on cookbook simplicity. For instance, one of the earliest commands Muggs learns is *come*. That is an obedience command (*recall*) and one you undoubtedly taught her before you read this chapter. Harness and leash training occur simultaneously with housebreaking, play sessions, and games. Muggs' education or training is cumulative. It is the sum of all knowledge that she accumulates through experience and invention, by watching other dogs, and by your specific teaching efforts.

Muggs is clever and will probably try her best to make you worship the ground on which she walks. She is an independent-thinking little rascal, often displaying scant desire to instantly obey. She is therefore more easily motivated by using food rewards. Fortunately, she has a great appetite! Trust forms when she is a puppy, so pay close attention to bonding. If you build Muggs' confidence in you, it is to you that she will turn when in doubt. Once she begins to focus on you and look to you for guidance, you're halfway home.

It is a rare dog that cannot be trained, and not to try is an error on your part. Muggs is a very intelligent, trainable canine. Her trainer should be a patient and knowledgeable person who knows her sensitivities and idiosyncrasies and who always acts with gentleness and kindness. If you have trouble fitting that description, get some help from a knowledgeable Pug trainer.

Training doesn't hurt, and errors leave no scars. She won't lose her spirit nor will she stop clowning and become melancholy. She will continue to exhibit her cleverness and personality throughout her lessons and will surprise you many times by modifying the exercise you have set forth or adding a unique end to the exercise. No matter what task you are teaching, your Pug's sense of humor will entertain you while you train her. Training is another step to socialization and Muggs' acceptance of her role in your pack.

A Pug Trainer's Role

You should keep a cool head in every situation and maintain alpha status and pack leadership regardless of the trainee's attitude. Trainers who specialize in training working or herding dogs might not recognize the sensitivities of tiny companion dogs or Muggs' clownish attitude. Likewise, trainers who work with hyperactive and hardheaded terriers or other breeds may be no better. A good Pug trainer has some special talents:

- Patience and consistency.
- Working knowledge of temperament, sense of humor, and sensitivity.
- Tackles one task at a time.
- Even temper and voice modulation.
- Persistence.
- The initiative to try new, proven training methods.

If you have the aptitude for the job, take it on. If you lack some of those talents, ask your breeder to recommend a Pug trainer who possesses the qualities you need. Then talk with that trainer. You can train your Pug better than anyone, but you might need help. Work with a professional trainer long enough to learn what you need to know.

Breed Truths

Intelligence is an inherited attribute that permits Muggs to learn by experience, example, and conditioning.

When to Start

Begin Muggs' schooling the day you pick her up from the breeder. Puppy bonding is part of her first lesson. You are her mentor and teacher, and it is never too early to start earning her trust. Each time you pick her up for a cuddle, you're reinforcing the mutual trust. At the same time, you're schooling her in the practice and reward for acceptable behavior and manners.

Now is the time to start. Before you do, plan your actions. Talk to Muggs' breeder, define success, and set realistic objectives. Keep your goal in sight, but make it achievable and never accept less.

Once you bring your puppy home, try to analyze her personality to determine what habits are most charming or pleasing to you. Many will be unexpectedly introduced when you don't have a pencil and paper handy, but more will show up each day. Record those habits. Notice what they are associated with and what brought them to your attention. Probably they

are stimulated by some activity or perhaps a word or words that were spoken. Take advantage of the habits that are natural to Muggs. When she sits up, immediately issue the command, "Muggs, sit up."

Conversely, when she displays some undesirable trait, discourage it quickly. Don't make a big fuss about it, or she will repeat it just to see if it causes a similar response from you. Use a simple "No!" spoken in a normal tone but curtly—a bit sharper than the word would be spoken in conversation. After giving that verbal reprimand, quickly walk away. Nothing gets a Pug's attention more than being ignored!

Use a bit of trickery when schooling Muggs. Make her think she's always right and never does anything wrong. Each time you walk out into the yard and she looks up, sees you, and begins to run toward you, take advantage of the situation. Call,

Helpful Hints

Don't give up! Teach Muggs that pleasing you and obeying commands pay off in both verbal and tasty rewards. Persistence will pay off. Soon your training tasks will be easier, and the joy of a well-trained companion is a fine reward.

"Muggs, come," and motion with your hand. When she reaches you, praise her, and give her a dry puppy kibble that is always in your pocket. Muggs will begin to focus without realizing that she is learning and concentrating on you. She's learning her name, the *recall* command, and the hand signal that accompanies it. She has won your approval and a tasty reward when she comes to you.

You've accomplished part of your training objective each time Muggs looks at you. Take advantage of that focus. Each time she looks at you, give her the verbal command and hand signal to come. When she arrives, give her some other task to perform, such as *sit*, and then reward her.

Don't starve her, but schedule your training sessions shortly before her feeding times. Not only is a hungry Pug more responsive to her handler, she is more apt to remember and appreciate commands that lead to tidbits. She will notice that it's always her best friend, the alpha pack leader, who fills her pan, gives her fresh water, grooms her, and gives her pleasurable moments of petting and kind words.

Ignore Mistakes

When Muggs digs in your vegetable garden, chews the hose, defecates in front of the yard swing, or otherwise makes errors in manners, ignore them. If you didn't leave the gate open, she wouldn't dig. If you hadn't left the hose out, she couldn't chew it. If you remembered to call her to her toilet area, you wouldn't have feces to shovel. Accept your share of the responsibility for her errors. After ignoring her for a reasonable time, toss a chew-toy to her. While she is not looking, fix the messes she made.

Muggs is smart. If she irritates you by digging up newly seeded lawn, she will remember how you respond. If you make a big fuss over the incident, she will begin to dig the next time you're working in the yard because she wants your attention.

Don't compound a mistake by calling her to you and then scolding her or shaking your finger in her face and telling her she's a bad dog. She won't know why you're so upset. She will always remember that she responded to your *recall* command and was rewarded with verbal abuse.

Muggs is a fine companion, but she isn't human. You are speaking to a dog. This little Pug has cognitive abilities, but she lacks abstract-thinking ability. Converse with her, but keep your dialog simple. Tell her things she can understand with no response required. If she's walking on lead and behaving well, reward her with an "Atta girl, Muggs." Watch her body language when you give her these words of encouragement. She'll toss you an appreciative glance or flick her ears, making it obvious she understands your approval.

When she misunderstands a command, make the correction softly. Tell her in a conversational tone, "Wrong," immediately followed by a demonstration of what action is correct. For example, when you're teaching her to sit, give the command, "Muggs, sit." If she lies down, don't make an issue of her error. Tell her quietly, "Wrong," and raise her front end and put her in a sitting position. Then stand her up, repeat the command, and reward her with praise and a tidbit when she performs correctly.

Illogical Commands
Never command Muggs to do a task that she is incapable of performing. A ridiculous example might best illustrate this. You lead Muggs to a 10-foot solid wooden fence and give her the command "Muggs, over." You're not only insulting her intelligence, you're giving her a foolish and confusing command that she can't possibly perform. Such action, if repeated often enough, will discourage an otherwise well-trained Pug and may irrevocably undermine your mentor-pupil relationship. Similarly, commanding Muggs to *heel* before demonstrating the meaning of that command will confuse and discourage her.

Don't put Muggs into situations where arbitrary responses are possible. For example, when she's running free in the backyard without the long training line attached to her harness, you give her the uncontrollable command "Muggs, come." Her response might be to come or to continue running, to change directions, to dawdle, or to sit down. Muggs decided to choose her response, and you find yourself unable to enforce the command. She suddenly assumes the alpha leadership role. Be sure you are always able to enforce each command you give with either a pull on the leash or a treat she won't refuse.

Training Techniques
There are many different techniques that can be used to train your Pug. In fact, you already use many of them even if you aren't aware you are doing so. Below are some of these techniques and how they are employed throughout your Pug's training.

Force sounds severe. When you encounter the word in training books, it has many inconsistent meanings. Force is sometimes a viable training method. When properly understood and applied, force has nothing to do with discomfort, pain, or abuse. Whether or not you like the word, several elements of force are implemented in practically all training. For instance, restraint is a type of force. Muggs certainly doesn't come to you and volunteer to put a restraint on her body. When you buckle her harness in place, though, you are forcing her to wear a shackle. You are forcing her to follow you when you snap on her leash. When you picked up Muggs for the first time, you turned her on her back and rubbed her tummy and chest, which is a type of force.

Habituation means to desensitize Muggs to a fearful event, such as thunder. Thunder can be recorded and played repeatedly in her presence, very softly at first and then at increasing amplitudes, while she sits at your feet being petted and reassured. After a few sessions, she learns to accept the noise through repeated exposure and your reassurances. That may be the same type of schooling used to prepare Muggs for Canine Good Citizen tests wherein she is exposed to honking traffic, clattering supermarket baskets, or people on crutches or in wheelchairs.

Associative Learning relates her action and your reaction. In its simplest form, Muggs comes to you and you pet her. She does something you like and you react pleasantly to it. She connects her action (running to you) to your reaction (petting and praise).

Negative Associative Learning or extinction occurs when a bad habit is extinguished by ignoring the unacceptable behavior. For example, Muggs chews the garden hose and you don't scold her or make a big issue of her action. Instead, you ignore her actions, put away the hose, and walk away. She interprets your reaction (ignoring her) as disapproval and will soon understand that any inappropriate behavior will get her nothing from you.

Punishment refers to a strong negative reaction to an inappropriate action. It might be your scolding, striking, or nagging Muggs. Punishment is a tool of ignorant and uninformed handlers. It is a technique used by someone who doesn't understand dogs and is attempted to dissuade the Pug from repeating an error. Punishment hardly ever succeeds and often compounds one mistake upon another. Muggs may concentrate on escaping training sessions, turning a deaf ear to commands, dragging her feet, and otherwise becoming uncooperative. Ultimately, she will run away and try to hide when you reach for her harness and leash. Muggs is overwhelmed and afraid to do anything when a command is given and the training goal is defeated. Repeatedly yelling or scolding is a form of punishment or even abuse.

Experience is invaluable, and Muggs continues learning throughout her life. By continual schooling, her experiences are broadened. More importantly, each positive experience expands her capacity to learn. Muggs' experience is multiplied and used in lessons that may or may not be connected with prior lessons.

Distractions can defeat a well-planned training session. Pick a spot where no interferences or distractions will bother you. Your backyard is perfect in good weather. In inclement weather, use a quiet room. Pug training is not a spectator sport and will progress more smoothly without an audience.

Treats are appreciated regardless of how miniscule those tidbits may be. The importance of an edible reward lies in the certainty and taste of the

treat, not its size. If you don't believe that statement, give Muggs a simple command and treat her with a tiny morsel of cooked liver. Then repeat the command but offer an unseasoned crouton for the treat. Her obvious disappointment in the taste will tell you that taste rules. The best treats are cooked chicken or red meat from your table. Cut those lean scraps into bites no bigger than a bean, bag them, freeze them, and thaw a few at a time. Do not leave treats at room temperature for more than an hour or two. Dried, commercial treats are convenient. However, they contain many undesirable preservatives and ingredients that Muggs never needs, such as sugar, propylene glycol, potassium sorbate, sodium nitrite, food dyes, and BHA.

Crate Training

Muggs' crate is her den, a quiet and peaceful haven where she naps. It is her refuge from noisy children, where she will always be left alone. A crate, or compact enclosure, is neither a lockup nor a place of punishment. It is an important tool that you can use in many different ways to aid in Muggs' training. It will provide her many rewards as well. Crate training, like any other training, will falter if anyone interferes, teases, speaks to Muggs, or causes any disturbance while she is being trained. Be consistent in your endeavor and success will follow, but never assume she's mastered the objective too soon.

- Place inside the crate a small rug or a folded towel and a favorite chew toy.
- Choose a time after Muggs has been playing hard.
- Put Muggs in the crate and give her a treat.

- Close and fasten the gate and quickly walk away, out of sight but not out of hearing.
- Leave her for 15 minutes.
- Re-enter the room, open the gate, turn immediately, and walk away. Do not speak to her or pet her.
- Ignore her actions and don't make a fuss over her after she has "escaped" from her crate; never give her a treat when you open the gate or otherwise acknowledge that anything out of the ordinary has happened.
- Leave the gate open to allow her access to her den. Several times during the day, repeat the crating technique.
- Place the crate in your bedroom at night so that she can retire at the same time you do.
- When she becomes restless during the night, open the gate, pick her up, carry her outside, and watch to see while she uses her toilet area. Then pick her up, put her back into her crate, and return to bed.

Housebreaking

Housebreaking a puppy is an idea that originated in human culture and is not included in the canine genetic makeup. Muggs has no idea what your intentions are when you begin the housebreaking task. Dogs have an instinctive desire to defecate and urinate at a distance from their home. All you must do is provide a suitable place, take her there frequently, and praise her after she has finished her eliminations.

Helpful Hints

The most difficult part of housebreaking is to first train yourself to act and react in time to prevent messes.

When Muggs arrives at your home, carry her from the car and set her on the ground in the pre-selected toilet area that can be some out-of-the-way corner of the backyard. The site should be protected from wind, perhaps the leeward side of a building or fence, and ideally should contain a few trees. You will be spending some time in the area. So if you have a big yard to choose from, pick a spot that is convenient. If possible, set up your X-pen in the toilet area, and take her to that pen each time she needs to go. Don't do or say anything to distract her sniffing. Stay with her in that portion of the yard for a while, quietly watching while she investigates the new smells. Don't remove her feces from the toilet area, and remember to bring her back to that spot until her excretory odors are firmly established in the area. Usually that takes only a few days.

Always carry Muggs to the toilet area when beginning her housebreaking. Do not ask her to walk. When she feels the need to evacuate her bladder

or bowel, she will squat, urinate or defecate, and continue walking. She won't realize that according to human design, she has put her wastes in the wrong spot.

The first step in housebreaking is to take Muggs to her toilet area. The next step is to keep an eye on a clock and follow these instructions.

- When you arise in the morning, physically carry her outside to her toilet area, put her down, watch for eliminations, and carry her or race her back to the house.
- After she's eaten each meal, pick her up and repeat the toilet trip.
- When Muggs is playing on the floor, watch closely for circling, sniffing the floor, and restlessness. When they are observed, pick her up and repeat the toilet trip.
- If she does not tell you by her actions that she needs to go out, repeat the toilet trip every two or three hours.
- Repeat the toilet trip immediately before retiring.
- If you must leave the house for a few hours, follow the same procedure that is used at bedtime. Take her to the toilet area before you leave, crate her with a small treat and a chewy toy, and leave. Repeat the toilet trip as soon as you return home.
- Never scold Muggs when she fails to perform appropriately.

Never expect immediate response and perfection. Sometimes when she's busily playing, she will get the urge to urinate or defecate and will relieve herself before you can intervene. When that happens, pick her up and make the toilet trip. Whether or not she performs, pick her up, carry her back to the house, and put her into her crate. Then clean up her mess using an appropriate cleaner, and deodorize the spot on the carpet with one of the special urine-deodorizing agents currently found on the dog equipment shelves of stores.

If pleasant weather encourages you and Muggs to be outside for playtime or training, always be sure to call her to the toilet area before you begin and just before you go back indoors. At night, she may awaken you with her restlessness and circling around and around in her crate. Alternatively, she may actually whine or make some other sound to call your attention to her discomfort. Don't delay, jump out of bed into your slippers, open her crate, gather her up in your arms, and hurry to the toilet area, regardless of the time or the type of weather. If you can't respond like a firefighter, it may take you a very long time to housebreak her, and it won't be her fault!

Molding and Polishing Habits

If Muggs does something new that pleases you, think fast! Name the incident, encourage it, and reward it with an edible treat. For instance, if she approaches you and sits down, immediately tell her "Sit." If she lies down, tell her "Down." If she stands on her hind legs, tell her "Up," and if she begins to turn around while on her hind legs, tell her "Dance." When you take her to the toilet area, stay with her. When she squats to urinate, say "Whiz." Call this training technique "command as she does." Keep treats in a pocket. When she performs on cue, reward her with verbal praise, petting, and a tasty tidbit. This positive good-habit reinforcement can work wonders. Conversely, negative reinforcement may be used in a similar manner. When she chews on a shoe, don't raise your voice, simply tell her "NO" in a sharp tone, then walk away immediately and ignore her for a few minutes. When she isn't watching, pick up the shoe and chastise yourself for leaving it out to be chewed.

Helpful Hints

Positive Attitude

Make Muggs' training sessions fun for both of you. Alternate playtime with training, and vary the time of day to suit your convenience so you will be in a positive training mood. Have at least one session per day, and strive for two or three.

Harness and Leash

Muggs' harness should fit tightly enough to prevent removal and loosely enough to allow two fingers to slide between her chest and the body strap of the harness. She will scratch at the restraint for a while. If you don't make a big issue of it, she will forget it in a few minutes. After putting on her harness, toss her chewy or stuffed toy and play with her for a few minutes. After she has worn the harness for 15 minutes, remove it until later in the day and repeat the exercise. After a few days of wearing the harness a few minutes at a time, it can be left on for longer periods. (The instruction for collar wearing is the same.)

The next step is the leash. Tie a 3-foot shoestring to Muggs' harness and let her drag it about for a few minutes, several times a day, for a few days. When she ignores the string, swap it for her leash, keeping hold of the loop. Coax her along with tiny treats while walking backward, keeping the leash

loose but not dragging. Continue with that training until she walks with you while you are holding the slack leash, and then encourage her to go ahead of you. Many times, both collar and leash training will be finished in two or three days.

Muggs' leash should never be jerked or tugged. When you are on a walk and she pulls hard, it probably is in response to a squirrel that just jumped from a tree or because she spots another dog down the street. In any case, she should be quietly told "Whoa." You should kneel beside her, reassuring her verbally and holding her still with your hand on her chest. If necessary, lift her and hold her in your arms until the excitement is over and she wants to continue her walk.

Leash Axioms

The road to success begins with getting Muggs' attention. Her focus must be on you when you start training.

- Call Muggs to you, put on her harness and leash (or you can try a show leash with a built-in collar), and speak to her in a quiet but authoritative tone.
- Never expect a miracle, and never spend more than five or ten minutes at each training session.
- Praise and reward Muggs every time she performs correctly, but ignore her errors without comment.
- Don't get angry or discouraged when she errs, and never scold her.
- Repeat the training sessions twice daily until a task is learned, and then move on to the next objective.
- Begin each session with a quick repeat or review of the previous day's work.

ACTIVITIES Training Tips

Practice various modulations of your voice. Find a tone that automatically tells Muggs that you are not just talking with her, and don't use that tone except when you are giving commands.

- Use the same training environment because the quietness of the area will add authority to your training.
- Put on her harness and leash for control.
- Use her name first, before the action command is spoken.
- Keep commands simple, use a single word if possible. Say, "Sit," not "Sit down," "Come," not "Come here."
- Make each command consistent, both in terms used and in word arrangement.
- The release word "OK" is the end of the task and should be said in a special, excited manner and tone.
- Give verbal and food rewards after she is released.
- After she successfully performs a task and is rewarded, lead her around the yard for a few minutes.
- The command should sound like this, "Muggs, sit" (she sits); "OK!" (release); "Good dog!" (reward and treat); lead her around for a minute; and repeat the command.

Correction

Correct Muggs' inappropriate actions immediately, but never overcorrect or scold. Never shout commands. For instance, if Muggs sits on command but springs back up before the release is given in anticipation of her treat, ignore the error and walk with her for a few yards. Stop and repeat the command. This time, though, place your hand on top of her rump, gently pushing and holding her in the sitting position. Then after she holds the *sit* for a brief time, give her the release "OK," reward, and go on to something else. Never end a training session on an error or negative note. If Muggs is having a tough day, finish the session with a task that she has perfected so that you can reward her, and she will be happy that she learned everything she was asked to do.

Helpful Hints

Alternatives to "No"

No is the most overused and sometimes abused command. "No" typically is yelled when you have no control over Muggs and are shouting from across the room. To many Pug owners, "No" means to stop whatever she is doing at that time. In theory, that's fine. However, it is applied to a multitude of actions, which minimizes the command's effectiveness. If you learn to use substitutes for *No*, both you and Muggs will be grateful.

Basic Commands

When Muggs has mastered the following tasks, she will be a better mannered companion. She will be happy with you because you are happy with her.

Recall or the *come* command was introduced when you taught Muggs her name. Start on the first or second day after she has come to your home and has eaten food from her bowl a few times.

1. With Muggs in the backyard and yourself in the kitchen, out of hearing and smelling distance, prepare a small portion of her favorite food in her bowl.
2. Step outside, show her the bowl, and say "Muggs, come!" in your command tone.
3. Kneel down, and place the dish on the ground.
4. After she has eaten the food, say "OK," praise her, pick up the bowl, and return to the kitchen.
5. If you repeat that exercise several times each day, you will have taught her to come when called.

Halt is taught to stop her progress, for instance, when you want Muggs to stop chasing the cat.

1. Begin by attaching her long line to her harness, and go into the back-yard training area.
2. Stand or sit and wait, and when she begins to walk away, say "Muggs, halt" in your command tone.
3. When she hesitates to see what you want, give her the *recall* command, "Muggs, come."

4. When she comes to you, praise, release, and reward.
5. If she doesn't halt, take up the slack on the long line to enforce the command.

Quiet is used to stop barking.

1. Say "Muggs, quiet!" in your command tone.
2. If she fails to stop, add negative enforcement to the verbal command. A quick shower of water from a spray bottle will do.
3. Then tell her "Muggs, come," and pet and praise her for coming to you.

Stop is the command to use if you want her to stop jumping up on your leg or the back door.

1. Say "Muggs, stop."
2. Reach down and hold her still.
3. After she has ceased the activity and relaxed, praise, release, and give her a reward.

Sit is used in a multitude of situations.

1. Position Muggs in a standing position, facing you with her rump a few inches from a wall.
2. Issue the command in your authoritative command tone. Say "Muggs, sit."
3. Hold a treat in your fingers, and move it toward and over the top of her head. Don't repeat the *sit* command.
4. She will follow the treat with her eyes and gradually sit.
5. After she sits, praise, release, and reward.

Stay is used to keep Muggs in a sitting or down position.

1. While she is sitting, hold a treat before her eyes and tell her "Muggs, stay!"
2. Hold the palm of your flattened left hand in front of her muzzle, fingers extended upward. If she doesn't relax, very slowly repeat the *stay* command. (If she relaxes, don't repeat the command.)
3. Continue to hold your flat left hand in front of her muzzle for about 30 seconds.
4. Drop your hand, praise, release, and reward.

Down is given when Muggs is in a standing or sitting position.

1. Tell her "Muggs, down."
2. Hold a treat in front of her muzzle. Show her your flattened left hand, held palm down above her head.
3. Slowly move the treat downward to the ground and backward between her front feet so she will lie down.
4. If she doesn't lie down, lower your open left hand to her back and let it rest there, exerting gentle pressure.
5. When she reaches the prone position and remains there for a few seconds, praise, release, and reward.

Up is a natural for all Pug beggars.

1. First give the *sit* command, and then tell her "Up."
2. Show her the treat held above her muzzle.
3. When she raises her forefeet from the ground, stretching to reach the treat, praise, release, and reward.
4. She may sit up in a begging position or stand on her back legs and wave her forefeet or all of the above. You can add further commands according to your desire.

Pug Tricks

Tricks are easy for a typical clownish, begging Pug. Remember to repeat each exercise two or three times in the first session and again at least once a day until she quickly and accurately responds. The most difficult factor in teaching tricks to Muggs is to keep her focused on your command. Many times the Pug will add one trick to another, until she has gone through her entire repertoire before she stops. She will do so quickly, trying each until she has all her treats gulped down. Most owners are so impressed with her memory that they forget what trick they originally asked her to do.

Shake or Gimme Five is natural for Muggs. Pugs automatically sit up.

1. When she sits up on her bottom to beg, kneel down in front of her with a treat firmly between your left thumb and index finger.

2. Grasp her right front foot with your right hand, and tell her "Gimme five."
3. Let go of the foot, release her with a verbal "OK," and reward with the proffered treat and praise.

Dance is another easy trick for your Pug.

1. When she is sitting up, raise the treat so that she can't quite reach it.
2. When she stands on her hind legs to increase her height, give the command "Dance," and move the treat in a circle over her upturned face. She will follow it by turning around and around.
3. Tell her "Good girl," release, reward, and praise.

Dead Dog is taught from a *down* position.

1. Give her the "Down" command and then the "Dead dog" command as you gently turn her over on her side and then onto her back.
2. Rub her abdomen for a few seconds to assure her that the position is what you are looking for.
3. Tell her "Good girl," release, reward, and add more verbal praise.

Bang is meant to be given when Muggs is walking across the floor.

1. Point your finger at her and sharply say "Bang."
2. When she looks at you and realizes you are speaking to her with a treat in your hand, she will appear puzzled but anxious to comply.
3. Then give her the "Dead dog" command, and she will catch on. Finish the exercise as usual.

Roll is also taught from a *down* position.

1. Give her the "Down" command, followed by the "Roll" command.
2. Gently roll her over.
3. Finish with verbal praise, release, and reward with more verbal reinforcement.

Bring Buy a tiny, stuffed bear, repeat "bear" several times, and give her the toy. Later the same day, set the stage.

1. Remove all toys from the toy basket except the bear. Call her to the toy basket and point to the bear in front of her. She will probably grasp it and carry it across the room.
2. You sit down a few feet away and give the command "Muggs, bring your bear." She may drop the bear and hurry to you, in which case you point to the bear, repeating the command.
3. If she doesn't pick it up, hand it to her, move back and repeat the command.
4. Once she has delivered the bear to you, praise, release, treat, and return the bear to the basket.

Helpful Hints

For many Pugs, praise and petting can be substitutes for edible treats, but curtailing all goodies from a Pug is tantamount to abuse.

The *bring* command can be used for each of her toys. Eventually she will learn to differentiate her toys by name and bring the item called for. Of course, as a Pug, she may pick up the first toy she finds and bring it; when she doesn't get the expected treat, she may begin bringing all her toys to you, one at a time.

You will undoubtedly use her tricks to entertain friends, but their real importance is giving your attention to Muggs. Any time you spend time with her, you are tightening the bond between you and your Pug, becoming a better owner and enforcing your role as a pack leader. Pugs are seen in circus acts and other forms of entertainment doing awesome stunts such as climbing ladders, walking on big balls, flipping, and hopping onto and off ponies, but those tricks are products of special, very trainable Pugs working for knowledgeable and experienced trainers. They consume hundreds of hours of patient practice. Start out with easily taught tricks and progress from there. Who knows? You might be on TV someday.

Activities

Most Pugs aren't super canine athletes. It is not because Muggs doesn't have the muscle mass or sufficient energy levels to perform athletic feats that leave audiences applauding. She is intelligent and has excellent coordination and balance that are so important to winning sporting events. It isn't that she is lazy or doesn't want to please her family. Everyone knows that she will capture all eyes and is the center of attention anytime she can move into the spotlight on the carpet.

Muggs simply isn't as vain and impressed with trophies and ribbons as some dogs. She has better things to do with her life than knocking herself out training for athletic contests. She is perfectly content in her home, entertaining family and friends in her clown suit, doing what Pugs do best—being funny, making the family laugh, and being a wonderful companion, loving and lovable pet, and very talented showoff.

Exercise Can Be Overdone

When Muggs sees you reaching for her harness and leash, she might actually smile. Pugs like adventure and will appreciate modest walks about the neighborhood. She may look forward to early morning and evening outings because it is cool. Like all dogs, she enjoys all the odors that emerge on crisp mornings from every new blade of grass. Exercise is necessary. Because of Muggs' small size, she can stay fit and healthy without hiking trails or Frisbee competitions. She can actually thrive on the exercise attained by following her favorite friend around your apartment, supplemented with a few minutes of play periodically.

Short Hikes

Muggs wasn't designed to be a great outdoor companion, and typically she is better off on grassy terrain or in the house. If a park or paved walking path is available, go for it. Even though she is a tiny dog, she will certainly enjoy your company on relatively short walks when the temperature isn't too warm. She is quite

CAUTION

Dusty Trails

Muggs should be protected from dusty environments whenever possible, and that means no dry trails for her. An inherent danger in walking outside Muggs' yard is her instinctive sniffing. Hunting breeds with their long muzzles are able to sniff out birds from their dusty habitats and rarely sneeze. Muggs' facial conformation makes dust her enemy, and her face is always just a few inches above the dirt. Dust may cause allergic swelling of her throat membranes and airways, resulting in croupy coughing and possibly choking that may aggravate the risk.

susceptible to heatstroke. When the weather is cool and she wants to accompany you on your next stroll, by all means, take her along.

Nighttime Excursions

If your work requires all your daylight hours, you still have weekends and evenings in which to exercise your little buddy. If you live in a hot climate, remember that exercise before the sun rises or after it sets is more comfortable than during the daytime. Visibility is a concern at these hours, but Muggs will be on lead, and her protection should be easily handled by putting reflective tape on her harness and leash. Shorten her leash after dark, and stay on well-

lit walkways. Don't allow her to enter into places where humans can't go. If you live in a rural area, she may have run-ins with skunks, porcupines, or other wild animals, and cars are always a serious threat. Keep her on a retractable leash that has a flashlight built into the handle.

Toys and Games

Muggs may like to play keep-away with small stuffed toys, balls, and rawhide chews. Those toys have warnings that accompany their use, so be cautious when selecting her playthings. Little soft, stuffed animals such as those that some of us have sitting atop our cabinets and computer furniture are just the right size. Unfortunately, most of those toys were not intended to be dog toys and are not tough enough to withstand the abuse that a Pug hands out. Some have glass eyes that Muggs will remove and swallow, so you should never give those to your little gal. Stuffed toys made for cats are a better choice. They may contain catnip, which can be removed, and the remaining toy will be more likely to survive Muggs' rough play.

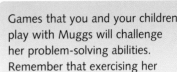

Breed Needs

Games that you and your children play with Muggs will challenge her problem-solving abilities. Remember that exercising her brain is as important as exercising Muggs' muscles.

Balls should be soft and pliable, but avoid the squeaky types. Innovative Muggs will find a way to remove the tiny metal squeaker valve and swallow it. She may suffer until the valve is removed from her stomach. She should never be allowed to play with a soft, yarn-filled ball because it will come apart when Muggs picks at it, and

hundreds of 1- or 2-inch yarn pieces will be found all over the floor. These fragments are tough to clean up, and Muggs and other small pets shouldn't eat bits of yarn that could cause serious digestive upset.

Pugs have well-developed scenting abilities, and Muggs may like the challenge of hide and seek. You can play hide and seek in the backyard when it is nice outside and in the house in inclement weather. Start out by using one of her tastiest treats. While your helper holds her, show the treat to her, let her smell it, and crawl backward into another room touching the treat to the floor as you go. Let her watch you and the treat disappear into the next room. When you are out of her field of vision, hide the bite of meat under the edge of a rug or behind a door. Then tell your helper to let Muggs go. The first few times she looks for the treat she will use only her eyesight and she may not succeed in finding it. If you let her smell the object each time before you hide it, she will soon catch on, use her scenting powers, and follow her nose straight to the hiding place. When she finds the treat, her reward is automatic, but your verbal approval and praise should always be given.

AKC Competitive Endeavors

Muggs is qualified to enter all events open to other members of the AKC Toy Group. You will occasionally see a Pug in an agility competition but probably not setting any records. Pugs often do very well in obedience trial competitions if you have sufficient patience to attend classes and practice daily. More than a few are seen in conformation shows, strutting their stuff and sometimes actually winning Best in Group.

FYI: A Note About AKC Resources

- American Kennel Club (AKC) is not a regulatory organization.
- AKC was founded in 1884 to promote breeding, showing, and canine companions for responsible dog owners.
- The organization's mission is to promote the ownership of purebred dogs and breeding those dogs for "form and function."
- AKC has no department that is responsible for locating reputable breeders and does not endorse or recommend specific breeders.
- AKC contact persons are appointed by each member breed club to provide referral services, but those contacts may not be breeders themselves.
- If you use AKC connections, the people to whom you speak are eager to take their time and knowledge to put you in contact with reputable breeders who may have puppies available.

Be patient and courteous. The people you call are experienced Pug owners, your neighbors, and fanciers. They may be away from their telephones and can take a few days to get back to you.

Agility Trials

Agility contests are excellent participation sports and are among the best canine spectator sports available to Americans. I heartily recommend that you attend an agility trial the next time one is held in your area. The competitors' personalities shine throughout the course, and love of the sport as well as the bond between contestant and trainer are displayed for every spectator to appreciate. Pug competitors are scarce in agility trials. However, obstacles are fitted to competitors' sizes, and it is entirely possible to join in that fascinating sport. If you want to find the rules and equipment needed to enter those trials, contact the AKC or your club secretary for details.

Obedience Trials

Many Pugs compete quite well in obedience trials. Formal obedience is an AKC canine discipline that requires extensive training, but Muggs can handle it. If she focuses on you when you speak to her and if she masters the Canine Good Citizen informal training, she will probably do well in obedience trials. Go to an obedience training session sponsored by your local dog club, and watch the owners and their dogs perform. That should tell you whether or not you and your companion are interested.

Canine Good Citizens

The Canine Good Citizen (CGC) test was accepted by the AKC in 1989 and since then has grown steadily in popularity. CGC certification is administered by a local dog club that will help you train Muggs, judge her accomplishments, and award her certification at the end of her training. Proof of the CGC certificate is required to pursue a therapy dog program such as the Delta Society or Therapy Dogs International. However, certification primarily proves that you have a well-mannered, obedient Pug. In the CGC program, no competition is involved among the dogs. An officer of the AKC-approved dog club will administer and evaluate Muggs' performance. If she passes, she will be awarded a certificate. If she fails, she is entitled to keep trying until she gets it right.

As the title implies, certification means that Muggs is well-mannered and trained to act with decorum and obedience. She can be taken for a walk without pulling and tugging at her leash. She doesn't embarrass her owner with her happy displays of excitement when meeting other dogs but may simply recognize a canine friend with a wag of the tail.

Muggs can be left loose in the house when guests arrive and will greet them courteously and respectfully without causing commotion, jumping up, or begging. A Canine Good Citizen displays acceptable behavior at all times and is a pleasure to be around. In other words, Muggs is a valuable pet, not a problem.

For most small, happy dogs, CGC training is the end product. It's where you want your companion to be, happy, and comfortable, and those accomplishments are quite sufficient. CGC training doesn't take the place of formal obedience training; however, Muggs may show aptitude in CGC training and welcome trying for the obedience title.

You can't "reason" with Muggs in any training program, regardless of how informal it is. Give a command, show her the response you expect, and insist that she obeys. Don't reward half-successes or almost-accomplishments, but don't nag either. Don't repeat commands endlessly. Exert yourself as the boss, but do so without verbal or physical abuse. Never yell at her or lose your sense of humor.

If there is a key to Good Citizen training, it is to gain Muggs' confidence and direct her concentration to you and what you are doing. You must let her know that you are serious, and she must focus on you at all times. Expect many Pug-like interruptions in your CGC training, but don't laugh or she may repeat her laughable error and then the day will be lost.

FYI: Therapy Pug at Work

Senior and handicapped residents of retirement communities, hospitals, rehab centers, and assisted living homes receive gigantic mental boosts from therapy dogs. A Pug that is comfortable on the laps or beds of those special individuals is always welcome. Muggs would probably be a great therapy dog, but she will need some specific training to perform in that role. Therapy dogs must:

- Be one year of age or more.
- Be appropriately vaccinated.
- Be of sound temperament and disposition.
- Be quiet and easily handled by strangers.
- Possess an AKC Canine Good Citizen Certificate (CGCC).

In addition, Muggs may be tested and rated by a certified evaluator from the therapy dog organization. The evaluator also measures the dog's behavior around people who use physical assistance, such as wheelchairs, walkers, or crutches. To find out more about therapy dogs, contact the Delta Society or Therapy Dogs Inc.

Muggs is evaluated in ten different exercises, all of which help to assure a dog is a good neighbor. There are no points involved; the scoring is a simple pass or fail evaluation. She is judged on essential, easily taught activities, which include the following exercises.

(1) Allowing a Friendly Stranger to Approach

This exercise demonstrates your control of Muggs when a friendly person is met on the street or in your home. She is expected to allow the person to approach without showing any aggression, such as barking or growling. She isn't marked down for wriggling and snorting in happy anticipation. However, she should maintain her position at your side and shouldn't jump up on the friend you meet. Training only requires Muggs to be comfortable with strangers, which means you must exercise her in public places.

To train, you need the help of several people with whom your dog is not familiar. When a friendly stranger approaches, tell Muggs to sit, and then step on her leash, holding her in place. After your helper greets you, shakes your hand, and talks to you for a few seconds, the person moves on, and Muggs is rewarded.

(2) Walking on a Loose Lead

Muggs is under control, walking on leash on either side. In the test, you will be given specific directions by the judge. You must turn left, right, reverse your direction, and stop, as the judge instructs. You are allowed, even encouraged, to talk to Muggs as you proceed through this exercise.

This task is usually taught to a puppy very early and is often a forerunner to the obedience exercise known as heeling. In the CGC exercise, Muggs' leash is kept loose. She doesn't necessarily walk on your left or keep her nose even with your leg, and she isn't required to sit when you stop.

(3) Walking Through a Crowd

This simple exercise is easily taught to Muggs as soon as she is leash trained. It requires no more from her than walking on leash in a public place. The judge asks you to take her alongside at least three people, some of whom are accompanied by their dogs. To pass the test, Muggs can show natural interest but no aggressiveness or shyness. She shouldn't demonstrate lack of control by tugging at the leash, barking, jumping up, or trying to play. You may talk to Muggs and encourage her during this part of the exercise.

Training for this test is about what you would expect. Walk Muggs on quiet streets of town, keeping her under control by means of your voice and the leash. Progress to busier streets as time passes, and obtain the assistance of some neighborhood children. Have them stand around, perhaps with a well-behaved dog on a leash. Take Muggs on her leash through this small crowd. If necessary, bait her with a treat when she shows interest in other dogs or people. Keep her interest focused on you by talking to her continuously.

(4) Sitting Quietly for Petting

This test is nothing more than demonstrating the tenets of a well-mannered dog. You will cause Muggs to sit on either side of you. Once Muggs has taken the sitting position, the judge will approach and pet her on her head and body. During the judge's handling, you can talk to Muggs, assuring her of your approval.

To pass the test, Muggs must not show shyness or aggressiveness. She must passively allow petting in the manner described after you have put her in the sitting position.

(5) Reacting to a Strange Dog

This exercise is a bit tougher for Pugs of all ages and is a real test of their ability to concentrate. Muggs is on lead, and you are walking across the floor or down the sidewalk. You meet a stranger who also has a well-behaved dog on a leash. When you meet, you stop, exchange pleasantries, shake hands, and continue your stroll. Ideally, Muggs will sit when you stop, but sitting is not mandatory.

Get and keep Muggs' focus. Obtain the help of several friends with well-behaved dogs. Ask them to take their dogs, on leash, up and down your sidewalk or across the yard. They should keep their dogs on the same side while walking, preferably their left side. As you approach a friend, gently tighten Muggs' leash a bit, so she is signaled of your awareness of the oncoming dog. This will shift her concentration from the dog to you. Talk to her, steady her, and keep her on your left side. Leash control is very important in this exercise, and a nylon leash with built in noose may be necessary.

In the first phase of training, pass the friend and dog without stopping. Keep Muggs' lead snug to control her actions. Speak to your friend, who should return the greeting. After passing them, reward Muggs according to her performance. If she only looked over her shoulder at the passing dog, she has made a good start and deserves a perfunctory reward. If she tugged at the lead, give her no reward. If she watched you, listening for commands, and hardly looked at either the person or dog, she should receive praise and perhaps a tidbit.

Repeat this training until Muggs passes dogs without a second thought. Then introduce the second phase, which is to stop and talk for a few seconds with the person, shake hands, and continue your walk. When you stop, it is an excellent idea to put Muggs in a *sit-stay* position.

(6) Reacting to a Distraction

In this test, the judge has several distractions from which to choose. Usually, he or she selects a sound distraction such as the slamming of a door. Another sound commonly used is dropping a book flat on the floor 10 or 12 feet behind Muggs. The judge also may knock over a chair 6 or 8 feet from Muggs or ask you to pass people who are talking loudly and making noise about 10 feet from Muggs.

Another part of the test is a visual distraction. It may be a person on a bicycle who rides about 6 feet from Muggs or someone pushing a rattling grocery cart passing about 10 feet from Muggs. The distraction might be a person running across your path or crossing your path on crutches, in a wheelchair, or using a walker.

In order to pass this test, Muggs may watch these happenings with natural curiosity. She shouldn't try to escape from them, bark, or show any fear or aggressiveness.

Training consists of regular exposure to these types of distractions. You can "stage" the sound distractions with the help of a friend who will expose Muggs to various sounds, including whistles and horns plus those mentioned above. By your voice and tone, let Muggs know she is safe. Control her actions with the lead. The sounds warrant her attention, but she should not be fearful of them. Keep her focus on you at all times.

Visual distractions are best handled by walking Muggs on streets where cars, bikes, skateboards, and motor scooters are buzzing about. Keep her a significant distance from these distractions at first. Then gradually change your path to bring Muggs closer. Never put yourself or Muggs in danger. Later, when you feel she has excellent concentration on your presence, your voice, and her leash, try walking through a supermarket parking lot where you can safely mingle with grocery carts being pushed back and forth. Remember, parking lots are dangerous places during busy hours.

If you ask, you will probably be allowed to take your Pug into a nursing home where she will regularly meet wheelchairs, walkers, and crutches. This is also a fine place to teach her to sit for petting. Many nursing home residents have a penchant for petting well-behaved dogs.

Keep up a steady conversation with Muggs while these distractions take place around her. Constantly reassure her. Signal her through her lead, letting her know she should stay at your side and not panic.

(7) Appearance and Grooming

The judge will approach and inspect Muggs to determine if she is clean, is well-groomed, and has a healthy weight and appearance. He or she then lightly grooms Muggs, inspecting her ears and picking up each foot in turn. Muggs is allowed to sit or stand during this exercise, and you are expected to verbally assure her at all times.

From the time you acquire Muggs, ask your family members, dog-owning friends, and other interested parties to participate in this good-manners training. A well-mannered dog should be amenable to grooming by anyone when you are present.

(8) *Sit* or *Down* and *Stay*

This is another test of owner control. It entails giving Muggs either the *sit* or *down* command, followed by the *stay* command. She is tested while wearing a 20-foot leash, which never leaves your hand. It measures your influence on your dog while you walk away from her and return to her side.

The test is begun when you are instructed to put your dog in the *down* or *sit* position and tell her to *stay*. You may touch Muggs to cause her to take the desired position, but you can't force her. The instructor then tells you to leave your Pug. You walk the length of the 20-foot line and then return to her and take your former position beside her. You are then instructed to release her from the *stay*.

(9) Praise and Interaction

This test immediately follows the previous two. It demonstrates your ability to calm Muggs after she has been rewarded with petting, scratching, and verbal praise when a *stay* exercise is finished.

The judge instructs you to release Muggs from the *stay* exercise. You give her a few "Good girls" or a scratch behind the ears to reward her for that behavior. Usually, she will be quite happy for the recognition and may wriggle, pant, or express happiness in other ways. After a few seconds of exuberant behavior, you are instructed to tell her "OK," or some other term to quiet her. You may tighten her leash, speak to her in a firm voice, or give her a signal with your hand, but her reponse should be to calm down immediately.

This calming task will probably be taught in dozens of ways during Muggs' housebreaking and manners training. By the time she is ready for this test, she should recognize an exuberant display is fine but that it must end within a reasonable time.

(10) Supervised Isolation

This tests the ability of Muggs to be left alone for three minutes without panic or showing excessive agitation. It is accomplished by tying her on a 6-foot line securely to a post or other immovable object and leaving her presence for three minutes.

Muggs will pass the test if she remains where you have tied her without chewing the lead, barking, whining, or pacing. She doesn't need to sit or lie down. She may move about, provided she remains calm and quiet and doesn't tug at her leash. She is expected to be interested in where you go and to be anxious for your return.

ACTIVITIES Fun Canine Games

Flyball

Flyball is a fascinating spectator event and is a team sport in which most dogs of every description can perform. Many flyball organizations are thriving all over America. Muggs probably wouldn't be interested and might need to take lessons from a Jack Russell or an Australian Shepherd.

Canine Freestyle Dancing

Freestyle Dancing is a beautiful spectator sport that should be right down a Pug's alley. Canine Freestyle is an event that Muggs might enjoy if you or a member of your family has a gift for dancing and choreography and if she is a very trainable student. The team consists of one human and one dog, who dance together in an intricate routine that is accompanied by music. If interested in this sport, you will find several organizations that will give you a wealth of information. Check the web site on page 157.

Frisbee

Frisbee is another spectator sport that draws very few Pug contestants, if any, but no lines are drawn to prevent a Pug from entering competition. Frisbee is an athletic canine event that includes running, jumping in the air, and sometimes bouncing off the handler's back to catch a Frisbee in the air.

Training consists of tying her for short periods of time out of sight while you walk around the house. Each time you leave, tell her to "Wait," and gradually increase the time you are away. It is very important for you to reward her with praise when she waits patiently for you. This task can be practiced in front of your home, in your backyard, or in any safe public place. No one is allowed to touch her while you are away, and distractions should be kept to a minimum.

Conformation Showing

The term conformation relates to the degree that Muggs conforms to the Pug Breed Standard, which is a description of a perfect Pug that is written by the Pug Dog Club of America. In a conformation show, each dog is compared to the official Pug Standard by AKC judges, considering form (structure and appearance), function (purpose), and temperament (disposition). The judge goes over the dogs with trained hands that pick up the slightest fault of gait, joint angulation, rib spring, tail set, and other bone structure.

Conformation showing requires training, because Muggs must be handled on leash at different gaits. She must be comfortable moving and being handled by a stranger (judge) in the show ring. The object of a conformation show is to select dogs that represent the best of both sexes of their breed that are entered in a show. Males and females of AKC registered dogs that have not been spayed or castrated may be shown. A show supports fanciers and breeders in their quest to breed and exhibit the best dogs available and thus move their bloodlines' progeny closer to perfection.

Dog show rules are quite structured and enforced. Before you consider entering such an event, you should study AKC's show regulations. Conformation showing begins with the puppy classes and progresses to the open classes. Each show proceeds step-wise to the ultimate Best of Show title. If Muggs wins first place in the Pug Open Bitch class, she is awarded 1 to 5 points, depending on the number of dogs entered in the class. These points are applied toward her Champion of Record title, which requires a total of 15 points. She would then be compared to the winner of the Open Male class, and the winner and Best of Opposite Sex would be decided. The winners of that competition progress to the next level, which is the Specials Class, wherein the winners are shown against AKC Champion Pugs. The winner of that class is proclaimed Best in Breed and goes on to the group showing, which judges the winners of each breed in the Toy Group against the other toy breed winners. The winner of the Toy Group advances to the final competition, and the winner of that class is declared Best of Show.

Helpful Hints

Join your local Pug club to learn more about conformation showing.

A commonly asked question is "How can several breeds that greatly vary in body structure, movement, and general appearance be judged against one another, especially when function as well as form is considered?" That question puzzles all novices and is usually answered, "The judge decides which of the various dogs comes closest to perfection for its breed, according to the written breed standard."

Leash Training

1 Place Muggs on a firm surface, and put the harness on her. The harness should fit tight enough to prevent removal and loose enough to allow two fingers to slide between her chest and the body strap of the harness.

2 Encourage play for the next 15 minutes until she stops scratching and trying to remove it.

3 Tie a 3-foot shoestring to Muggs' harness and let her drag it about for a few minutes. Repeat those steps several times daily for a couple of days.

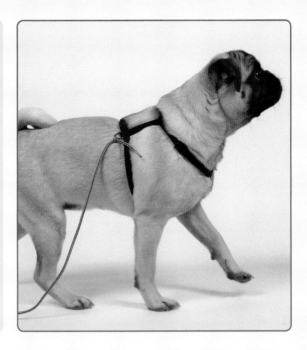

4 Swap the shoestring for her leash, and keep hold of the loop. While walking backward, coax her along with tiny treats, keeping the leash loose but not dragging. Within a few days, she will be eager to join you for walks.

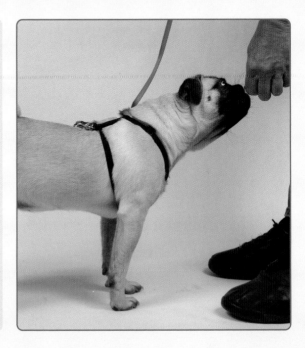

The *Sit* Command

1 Position Muggs in a standing position, facing you with her rump a few inches from a wall.

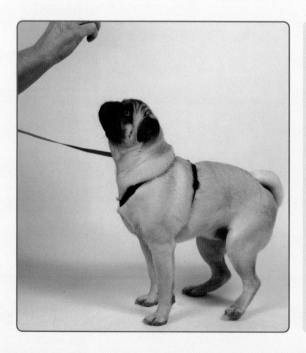

2 Tell her in your authoritative command tone "Muggs, sit."

3 Hold a treat in your fingers, and move it toward and over the top of her head. Don't repeat the *sit* command.

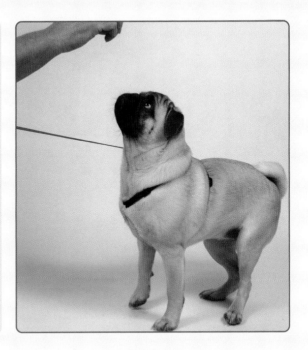

4 She will follow the treat with her eyes and gradually sit. After she sits, praise, release, and reward.

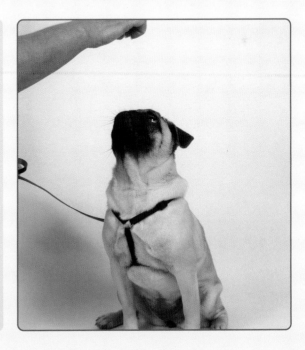

The *Stay* Command

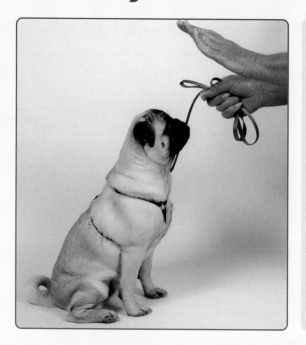

1 While Muggs is sitting, hold a treat before her eyes and tell her "Muggs, stay!"

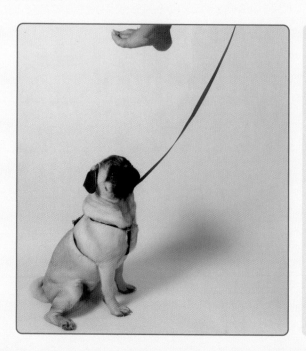

2 Hold the palm of your flattened left hand in front of her muzzle, fingers extended upward. If she doesn't relax, very slowly repeat the *stay* command. (If she relaxes, don't repeat the command.)

3 Continue to hold your flat left hand in front of her muzzle for about 30 seconds, and then drop your hand, praise, release, and reward.

4 After Muggs has the idea, practice extending the *stay* time, gradually backing away from her until you reach a reasonable period, about 1 or 2 minutes.

101

Chapter Six

Pug Health and Nutrition

Y ou are Muggs' owner, the person who bought her, the one who insisted that this little ball of charm and mischief is to share your home for the next 15 years. Therefore, you make the decisions about her veterinary care and diet. That is an awesome responsibility, but you don't need specialized training. If you communicate closely with Muggs, you should be able to recognize her healthy condition, and signs of disorders will be obvious to you. Common sense and close observation are the only requirements. Most of the health conditions described hereafter will never be seen, but being forewarned is better than playing catch-up.

Breed Needs

Regular, personal examinations at home are practical components of preventive medicine.

Pug Health

Muggs' preventive medicine plan begins with an understanding of her early physical development. This 10-inch, 14-pound dog has a life expectancy of 15 years but reaches maturity quite early. Muggs' sexual maturation is complete (and her first heat may be predicted) when she is just six months of age, which is earlier than uninformed owners expect. You should consider that when planning spay or neuter surgery.

You should keep up with Muggs' health needs on a regular basis. Stay abreast of the changes in her life by performing regular weekly examinations. Spread a bathtub mat on a handy tabletop, lift her to the table, and begin the exam.

Temperature Take Muggs' body temperature rectally using a plastic digital thermometer. If elevated 2 degrees or more, it should be rechecked after an hour's rest. If still elevated and you find no other symptoms, such as discussed below, consult your veterinarian.

Pulse Muggs' normal pulse rate should be counted early in the morning, when she is quiet, is not excited, hasn't been running, and isn't displaying signs of illness. To do this, place one finger, pressed lightly, on the inside of the

FYI: Pug's Normal Values

Temperature	101 to 102°F
Pulse Rate	Varies from 80 to 140 beats per minute, depending on age and activity level
Mucous Membranes	Bright pink tongue and ocular membranes
Eyes	Clear cornea (transparent front part of eyeball) with no yellow or greenish discharge
Eyelids	Flat against the eyeball, not rolled inward or drooped downward
Skin	Supple, clean, without redness or hairless areas
Wrinkles and Nose Roll	Not reddened, dry to touch
Ears	Canals dry and no excessive wax, bad odor, or visible discharge
Teeth	Clean, white, and solid
Weight	Between 14 and 18 pounds
Chest	Ribs easily palpable with a thin fat covering
Abdomen	Full, but not distended, with no distinct tuck behind ribcage
Tail	Tightly curled and quite animated
Legs	Joints smooth and not sensitive when palpated
Feet	Pads smooth and supple, toes held tightly together
Toenails	Toenails not overly long, broken, or torn
Digestive System	Excellent appetite and normal bowel movements
Respiratory System	Breathing normally and no coughing, wheezing, or sneezing
Genitals	Clean, pink, slight clear discharge is OK
Urine	Bright yellow and clear

hind leg about halfway between abdomen and stifle (knee) joint. If you have difficulty finding the right spot, ask your veterinarian to show you on your next appointment. Count the number of beats and record it. If the pulse is abnormally high or racing, keep Muggs quiet for a few minutes and try again.

Mucous Membranes Pugs may have pink oral membranes, or they may have pink tongues with black gums and black palates or any other combination of pink and black. Black membranes are difficult to evaluate. Usually a sufficient amount of pink membranes will be found to check for paleness or bluish colors that typify loss of blood, shock, or other serious illness. If those normally pink membranes are cherry red, they may signify heatstroke or poisoning and should be considered a sign of real trouble. Call your veterinarian immediately.

Eyes Yellow or greenish ocular discharge may be a sign of conjunctivitis, inflammation, or infection of the mucous membranes surrounding the cornea. If this occurs, clean the affected eye with a cotton ball moistened with tepid tap water. If discharge is repeatedly present, consult your veterinarian. Don't use human eyewash or medication unless you are advised to do so by Muggs' veterinarian. Some ophthalmic solutions and ointments contain steroids that inhibit healing of corneal scratches.

Breed Truths

Your Pug, like a child, thrives on personal attention. Monitor Muggs' appearance, appetite, attitude, and activity, all of which are signs of general health.

Eyelids A hereditary eyelid deformity called entropion may cause Muggs' eyelid(s) to roll inward, resulting in her eyelashes irritating her cornea(s). The irritated cornea becomes inflamed and infected, which results in ocular discharge. If in doubt, consult your veterinarian.

Skin Muggs' skin normally has a pliable feel and smooth texture. It should be clean, and no reddened or hairless areas should be apparent. Grasp a fold of skin between your fingers and thumb, lift upward an inch, and release—it should snap back immediately. If it remains pinched up for more than a heartbeat, it is a sign of dehydration and should be reported to your veterinarian.

Wrinkles If Muggs' "nose roll" or any other body wrinkle has a bad odor, is reddened, is sensitive to touch, or is damp, you have reason for alarm. If any of these are found, clean the skin in the wrinkle with a cotton ball slightly moistened with 2 percent hydrogen peroxide, dry with a gauze pad, and then apply a thin layer of triple antibiotic ointment. Repeat the treatment every 8 to 12 hours. Alternative therapy is the use of an astringent instead of ointment. After three or four treatments, if the inflamed tissue isn't responding to therapy, consult your veterinarian.

Ears An ear canal that is moist, with wax or pus exuding, or that has a bad odor, may be in trouble. It could be caused by foreign material in the canal, ear mite infestation, or ear infection (*Otitis externa*). Clean the external canal with cotton balls moistened lightly with 2 percent hydrogen peroxide. If the abnormality persists, if Muggs tilts her head, if she scratches at the ear, or if a foul odor persists, consult your veterinarian.

Teeth A Pug's short, blunt muzzle and slightly undershot lower jaw often predispose her to dental problems. With the lips pushed back from the teeth, inspect and feel the teeth with your index finger and note any that are loose or yellow. Yellow teeth may indicate early plaque or tartar formation or periodontitis (inflammation or bacterial infection). Retained baby teeth are

fairly common in Pugs. In that case, the adult teeth erupt through the gums behind the deciduous (baby) teeth. For a time, Muggs will have a double set of teeth. That situation may involve one or several teeth. When double teeth are noticed, wriggle the baby teeth with your finger. If one wriggles easily, you can probably ignore it and it will be shed naturally. If the baby tooth happens to be a canine tooth (fang), which is solidly positioned behind the permanent tooth, it will invariably require veterinary extraction under anesthesia. Prevent or treat yellow teeth by initiating a daily or semi-weekly brushing program. (See the *Grooming Your Pug* chapter.)

Weight Muggs should weigh between 14 and 18 pounds. Feel her ribs with your fingertips. If her ribs are deep beneath a heavy layer of fat and your fingertips have trouble finding them, she is probably overweight and should be on a diet. If they are easy to palpate and are not covered with a thick fat layer, she is probably not overweight. Obesity is dangerous to any Pug! Excessive fat is often associated with metabolic disorders and can shorten the life of your best buddy!

Abdomen Muggs' abdomen should be supple. It should feel firm but not tight, hanging, or distended. Her abdomen should make a smooth transition from the rib cage. No tuck up should be apparent. A drum-tight abdomen or one that is hanging or tender to palpation is abnormal.

Tail Muggs' tail is carried over one hip. If it hangs loosely or its curl isn't perpetually wiggling in a vain attempt to wag, she may be unwell. If the tail abnormality persists, take her temperature, and consult her doctor.

FYI: Dietary Behavior or Apathy

Muggs is a beggar! She would like to eat people food and would appreciate a continuous source of treats each day, but those would definitely upset her nutritional balance. Don't yield to her sad eyes, sitting up, or other automatic begging behaviors. Her nutritional demands must always be met, but that does not mean giving her whatever she wants and all she wants. Never change her diet on a whim. If you see a need for change, proceed gradually and thoughtfully.

Occasionally Muggs may be listless and not anxious to eat her meal. She might pick up her food and roll it around in her mouth or spit it out. These are signs of illness, and you should pay strict attention to them. Check her mouth, gums, and teeth; take her temperature; and observe her actions closely. If her temperature is greater than 103°F, call her veterinarian. Place her in a small pen or her crate until the problem is solved to observe whether or not she vomits or has diarrhea.

Legs Palpate all joints of Muggs' legs for signs of tenderness, swelling, calluses, or injuries. Be particularly observant of her stifle joints. The patella (kneecap) sometimes slips out of its track and causes intermittent lameness that should be reported to your veterinarian.

Feet Examine her pads for wounds. If Muggs is licking and fussing at a non-bleeding pad wound, clean the pad with gauze and mild soap, apply a thin coat of triple antibiotic ointment, and bandage the foot with two or three layers of gauze bandage. Apply a layer of adhesive tape over the gauze and up onto her ankle. Change the bandage after 24 hours or sooner if it gets wet or any swelling is apparent above the bandage. If she licks and chews the bandage, apply a mist of bitter apple (available at pet supply stores). Continue to protect the pad injury for three or four days, and then leave it unbandaged.

Toenails If any nails are broken, twisted, turned, or clicking on the floor, a nail trimming is in order (see Chapter 7). If Muggs' nail is broken but not bleeding, it needs no attention. It will remain sensitive for several days but shouldn't cause serious lameness. If her nail is raggedly broken, trim it with a nail clipper, canine nail file, or emery stick. If the nail injury is fresh and oozing blood, cauterize with a dampened styptic shaving stick or with a commercial blood stopper from the pet supply store. Kennel Muggs for an hour to be sure the bleeding has stopped, and limit her activity for the rest of the day.

Vomiting or Diarrhea Intestinal upset is usually caused by eating foreign material. Take Muggs' temperature, and gently palpate her abdomen. If her abdomen is tender, if she is vomiting repeatedly, if the condition has persisted for more than 12 hours, if blood is apparent in the vomit or feces, if she has a fever, or if she is displaying pain or lethargy, consult your veterinarian. If none of those signs are present, you may choose to initiate home management. For vomiting, withhold all food and water for 24 hours. If she appears terribly thirsty, put two ice cubes in her water dish. An hour after the ice cubes are gone and if no vomiting is seen, two more cubes can be offered at hourly intervals. After the 24-hour fast, prepare a bland diet mixture of ⅓ cup of cooked and drained lean hamburger, ⅓ cup of dry-curd cottage cheese, and ⅓ cup of cooked white rice. Feed a small amount (about ¼ cup total) every six hours. If recovery is uneventful and Muggs eats and doesn't vomit, mix the bland diet ½ and ½ with regular food and gradually return to regular feeding. If diarrhea without vomiting is the only problem, withhold food for 24 hours. During the fasting period give Muggs one tablespoonful of kaolin-pectin mixture (available at natural food stores) every four hours for four doses. After the fasting period, feed the bland diet until stools are normal, and then gradually change back to regular feeding.

Respiratory System Repeated and unproductive coughing or sneezing may be caused by inhaled smoke, dust, or pollen. The condition probably will begin to right itself within a day after the irritation is eliminated from Muggs' environment. If symptoms persist, if a yellow or greenish nasal discharge accompanies her cough or sneeze, or if she becomes lethargic or feverish, take her temperature and consult your veterinarian.

Genitals A slight, white or clear discharge is normal from a male Pug's prepuce. Any significant colored discharge should be noted and reported to your veterinarian.

Urine If Muggs' urine is bloody, dark brown, contains sediment, or is colorless, consult your veterinarian. Those signs are commonly associated with cystitis (bladder infection), cystic calculi (bladder stones), nephritis (kidney infection), kidney failure, or metabolic disorder.

Administration of Medicine
Lift Muggs to a no-slip mat on a table and have an assistant steady her.

Liquids
1. Insert your left thumb inside Muggs' right cheek where the upper and lower lips form a pouch.
2. Grasp the pouch with your thumb and index finger, and gently pull it forward about half an inch.
3. With your right hand, insert the medicine dropper alongside your thumb, between her lower teeth and cheek.
4. Squeeze the dropper bulb, and withdraw your thumb.
5. Firmly but gently hold Muggs' mouth closed and the liquid will flow through the teeth, onto the tongue, and be swallowed.

CHECKLIST

First Aid Kit

✔ Rubbing alcohol
✔ Bandage roll
✔ Bitter apple
✔ Cotton balls
✔ Cotton swabs
✔ Emergency veterinary clinic phone number
✔ Gauze pads
✔ Hemostats or blunt tweezers for removing ticks, thorns, and stickers

✔ Hydrogen peroxide, 2 percent
✔ Kaolin-pectin mixture, without aspirin
✔ Regular veterinarian's name, address, and telephone number
✔ Organic iodine solution
✔ Poison control telephone number
✔ Blunt scissors (blunt-blunt)
✔ Adhesive tape
✔ Digital, plastic thermometer
✔ Triple antibiotic ointment or cream

Tablets or Capsules

1. Place a teaspoon containing butter or cheese dip on the table.
2. Grasp Muggs' muzzle firmly between your left index finger and thumb.
3. Gently squeeze inward with your fingers, forcing her cheeks between her upper and lower teeth so her mouth will open.
4. Hold the pill between your right index finger and thumb. As her mouth opens, place the pill on the top of her tongue, as far back as possible.
5. Immediately remove your right hand, holding her muzzle loosely closed with your left hand.
6. Quickly coat your right index finger with butter and wipe it off on Muggs' nose. Her tongue will immediately flick out to lick off the butter, and she will swallow the pill.

Choosing Your Veterinarian

On those rare occasions when you need veterinary help, the obvious choice is a local veterinary practitioner with whom you and Muggs are compatible. Nearly all veterinarians have abundant scientific knowledge and practical experience in canine medicine. Muggs' veterinarian must also possess knowledge of a Pug's idiosyncrasies, which are somewhat different from other breeds' needs.

In addition to proper equipment, the veterinarian you choose should possess:

- Effective tableside manner, including soft speech and gentle hands
- Great sense of humor
- Proper technique to hold and examine a 15-pound, happy, exuberant Pug
- Understanding of a Pug's genetic conditions

To find your veterinarian, visit more than one animal hospital, take a tour, talk to the staff, and meet the clinicians. If possible, observe the doctor examine a Pug or another toy breed. Watch the clinician's technique. He or she should be gentle but firm, calm, relaxed, and at one with the patient. Watch the dog being examined. If she continually squirms and whines, watch the veterinarian's reaction.

Ask questions. If the clinician smiles a lot and pets the patient while answering your questions, if his or her answers are thoughtfully formed, and if consideration is given to the size and disposition of the patient in each response, you're probably in the right hospital. If the practitioner needs help to calm an exuberant patient on the table, if he or she answers your questions hurriedly in a general way that indicates "all dogs are cookie cutter creations," or if he or she is rushed, fidgety, or unsure, you may be in the wrong hospital.

During your clinic tour, look at the general cleanliness of the facility. Sniff for rancid odors (excluding doggy odors and recent accidents). Look for a well-equipped laboratory, clean uniforms on the staff, and evidence of organization that indicates a smooth-running animal hospital. The operating room should contain a modern anesthesia machine and patient monitors, and the room should not be crammed with extraneous equipment or kennels. Check the dog wards for tidiness and appropriate kennel size.

Ask about referrals to specialists in case you need one. Specialists often are located in a large city or in a veterinary college. If Muggs needs to see a cardiologist, ophthalmologist, or other specialist, your veterinarian should know where to find them.

Ask a staff member to see a fee schedule if one is available, and if not, ask if fees are itemized. Inquire about the cost of a routine well-dog examination. Ask about neutering and vaccination charges and about fecal examination fees. Ask how heartworms, ticks, and fleas are controlled in your area. Consider using the hospital only if you're comfortable there and feel that the resident veterinarian(s) can be trusted with Muggs' health care.

Helpful Hints

Insurance

Health insurance is available for Muggs. If you are interested, ask your veterinarian how to subscribe. Some plans are reasonably priced and cover some of your Pug's health needs. Be certain that your veterinarian accepts the insurance you buy.

CAUTION

Sometimes a Pug is poorly served by a veterinarian who has plenty of medical knowledge but lacks experience with an outgoing, fun-loving little dog.

FYI: Ongoing Vaccination Debate

A veterinarian may administer a multivalent (combination) vaccine that protects against several diseases or a series of monovalent (single) vaccines administered a week or 10 days apart. The monovalent product allows your veterinarian to determine whether or not a vaccine causes a reaction. The downside of that technique is that Muggs will need to see your veterinarian more frequently, and several monovalent vaccines will undoubtedly cost more than a single dose of a combination vaccine. In either event, booster vaccinations are scheduled to assure that Muggs continues to produce a safe level of active immunity.

Vaccines and How a Vaccine Works

A vaccine is prepared by one of several means. A killed virus vaccine usually has lower antigenicity (ability to elicit an immune response) than a living, attenuated (reduced potency) virus vaccine. Either type has a place in immunizing Muggs, but vaccination must be administered before she is exposed to the pathogen.

Passive Immunity

Muggs' mother's antibody level is influenced by many factors, such as her past vaccinations, nutritional state, disease exposure, and general health. Some of those antibodies pass through the pregnant dam's placenta to each fetus, and each pup also receives additional antibodies in the dam's colostrum (first milk). Those maternal antibodies protect Muggs for a limited time, but they eventually disappear. That temporary protection is called passive immunity.

Muggs' immune system is not functioning at birth. Any neonatal (newborn) pup has only a very slight ability to produce her own immunity. Passive immunity antibodies soon begin to disappear from Muggs' bloodstream. When they fall below a protective level, her health is at risk.

Vaccinating Muggs while her maternal antibodies are present will result in some vaccine particles being neutralized by those antibodies. Thus, a narrow vaccination window exists after Muggs' maternal antibody levels are nearly depleted but before she is at risk of exposure.

Veterinarians have researched and studied this phenomenon extensively to try to determine the best time to vaccinate a puppy. However, the exact *best time* to vaccinate all puppies is unpredictable because each dam-and-pup pair is unique unto itself. According to veterinary immunologists, most, if not all, of the passive immunity is gone from Muggs' bloodstream by eight weeks of age.

Active Immunity

Active immunity occurs when Muggs' immune system is triggered by any means to produce antibodies. A vaccination or an exposure to a live, virulent

pathogen will trigger the system to produce antibodies. If the patient doesn't succumb to the disease, long-term immunity will result.

When to Vaccinate

Arbitrary vaccination schedules are generally obsolete. Muggs should most certainly be vaccinated. However, the frequency at which vaccines are given should be structured to fit her individual needs. Vaccinations also should be considered according to the region of the world in which she resides and diseases that are endemic (prevalent) in that region, as disease exposure potential varies according to the area in which you reside or to which you travel.

Breed Truths

Antigens and Antibodies

An antibody is a specialized protein molecule that is produced by lymphoid cells, which are part of Muggs' immune system. An antibody destroys or neutralizes a specific antigen, which may be a disease-causing particle such as a virus or bacterium (pathogen). Each antigen has its own antigenicity (disease-causing capacity), which is the potency of the antigen.

Boosters

Canine vaccine manufacturers often combine several products, and the combination is less expensive than the sum of individual vaccines. Combination vaccines are available to protect against any or all of the following: canine distemper, hepatitis, leptospirosis, parainfluenza, parvovirus, and coronavirus. Tracheo-bronchitis (*Bordetella*), lyme, and rabies vaccinations and boosters are usually administered individually.

Some vaccines confer longer lasting immunity than others. For example, a leptospirosis immunizing agent confers shorter immunity than distemper vaccine, therefore lepto vaccine (if used) should be administered more often than distemper vaccine. A single dose of lepto vaccine may cost more than a dose of a combination product that contains both distemper and lepto vaccines.

Some veterinarians use blood tests that provide antibody levels to determine which vaccine is actually needed. Unfortunately, each test may cost significantly more than a combination product vaccine booster. Consider your veterinarian's experience, the risk, and the cost, but please immunize Muggs before exposure to other dogs.

Canine Diseases and Conditions

There are many canine specific diseases that all dog owners should be aware of. Some can be life threatening and require immediate treatment. Others are less threatening but must be diagnosed and treated accordingly.

Chocolate (Theobromine) Poisoning is not hereditary and is rarely fatal. It needs to be discussed because it usually occurs in a treat freak like Muggs. Even in small amounts, chocolate may cause illness.

Dark chocolate or milk chocolate contain less theobromine than baking chocolate, but the former products are more available. Signs of chocolate poisoning are nervousness, vomiting, diarrhea, and urinary incontinence. If Muggs finds and consumes a big supply of chocolate in any form, the safest therapy is to induce vomiting or administer activated charcoal suspended in water. Charcoal is given orally, at the rate of 1 gram of charcoal per pound of Muggs' weight. Vomiting may be induced by oral administration of 1 teaspoonful of 2 percent hydrogen peroxide or by placing a pinch of table salt on the back of Muggs' tongue.

CAUTION

It would be necessary for a 20-pound dog to eat a pound and a half of baking chocolate to be fatal, but it takes much less to make a 15-pound Pug quite ill.

Hot Spots Flea bites or other irritations or allergies may cause localized skin irritations. Muggs licks or scratches the spot, her saliva dampens her coat, and she continues bothering it until the skin is grossly reddened and serum is oozing. Soon bacteria begin to multiply in the moist, warm, damp lesion, resulting in a hot spot. Therapy is usually straightforward and may include oral anti-inflammatory medication or injection, shaving the lesion, and application of antibiotic creams, drying agents, and possibly a product such as bitter apple to inhibit Muggs' licking.

Kennel Cough (*Bordetella bronchiseptica*) Uncomplicated kennel cough is rarely fatal. It is spread by airborne particles, often from a sneezing and coughing infected dog. It causes a chronic, honking cough that may continue for many weeks. No specific therapy will cure kennel cough, but various medications may relieve some symptoms. Ignoring the condition may lead to complications from viral pathogens, such as parainfluenza or distemper virus, which may be fatal.

Heatstroke This is prevalent in short-muzzled dogs such as Muggs. Heatstroke can even occur in mild weather if a Pug is closed in a car.

Be aware that many municipalities have laws in effect that address canine heatstroke and attach severe penalties. When an automobile is sitting with sun shining through a window, it becomes a virtual oven, reaching temperatures of 140°F or higher in a short time. An enclosed dog's temperature may quickly reach 105 to 110°F or higher. Respiration becomes rapid and labored, panting begins, and thick, stringy saliva exudes from her mouth. Oral mucous membrane color changes from pink to bright red. It soon turns pale and bluish and then she becomes comatose. Without immediate treatment, she will die.

Treatment involves cooling her with water from a garden hose or placing her in a tub of cool water. Do not use crushed ice or ice water, because the ice will cause skin blood vessels to constrict, delaying the water's cooling effect. If she is awake, encourage drinking water. Cool water enemas may be used to bring down her body temperature, but intravenous fluids and other shock therapy are most effective. Unfortunately, heatstroke is a dire emergency and rarely allows owners the time to seek professional help.

Never leave Muggs in your car, even for five minutes, unless the car and air conditioner are both running and you have plenty of gasoline in the tank. Be certain that she has plenty of water in her yard and in your home. If she is left in her backyard for extended times without sufficient shade and drinking water, she is also at risk.

Canine Distemper (CD) (Dog Plague or Hard Pad) remains a significant threat to all American canines. CD kills many dogs, can't be cured, and is easily transmitted. It is caused by a virus that attacks a dog's respiratory tract, intestinal tract, and brain. The reservoir of infection for CD exists in cities' stray dog populations and wild carnivores such as coyotes, wolves, ferrets, raccoons, bats, and foxes.

Signs of CD may include fever, anorexia, lethargy, dehydration, diarrhea, and vomiting. A yellow or green ocular discharge and coughing are often present. When a young, unvaccinated puppy contracts CD, it often dies suddenly without displaying any symptoms. Permanent damage in those dogs that miraculously survive the disease include hardened footpads, tooth enamel deficiencies, and neurological signs such as blindness or twitching of extremities.

Infectious Canine Hepatitis (ICH or CAV-2) is caused by canine adenovirus-2, hence the abbreviation CAV-2. It is a systemic, usually lethal liver infection that also destroys an infected puppy's resistance to other diseases. Signs of CAV-2 are similar to those of CD, including sudden death of unvaccinated puppies.

Leptospirosis (Lepto) is a devastating disease whose carriers are water rodents and is often transmitted by drinking or swimming in contaminated river or lake water. It is caused by bacteria-like organisms called spirochetes, which can destroy an affected dog's kidneys. Signs of lepto include lethargy, anorexia, thirst, rusty-colored urine, diarrhea, and vomiting. Affected dogs sometimes walk with a peculiar, stilted gait.

Parvovirus (Parvo) is a contagious, often fatal disease that is spread by feces of an infected dog. The virus is highly resistant to disinfectants and may survive for many months in dried dog feces. Signs of the disease are high fever, bloody diarrhea, vomiting, dehydration, and cardiac complications. Intensive therapy can be effective, but the disease's side effects may be significant.

Coronavirus is typically seen only in puppies and is similar to parvo in that both usually cause bloody diarrhea and vomiting, general malaise, and death in many affected puppies or adults.

Lyme Disease (Borrelliosis) is a systemic bacterial disease that is spread by blood-sucking parasites, such as deer ticks. The infection causes nonspecific, generalized malaise; fever; joint swelling with pain; lymph node swelling; and other vague signs. Lyme disease may affect humans. It sometimes can be successfully treated with long-term, intensive antibiotic therapy.

Periodontitis is the result of bacteria, saliva, and food particles collecting between your Pug's teeth and gums and the formation of plaque on the teeth that, in time, becomes tartar. That collection of debris and bacteria, if not removed, causes inflammation and infection of gums called periodontitis. Periodontitis can cause tooth loss. In a worst-case scenario, the infection can be spread by the bloodstream to the heart, liver, or kidneys. A manufacturer of a new vaccine has been awarded a conditional USDA license (meaning that the product has met the purity, safety, and efficacy expectation) for this product. It is available to veterinarians at this time and is commonly called the porphyromonas vaccine.

Ehrlichiosis (tick fever) is another serious bacterial disease and is transmitted by the brown dog tick. It is manifested by nosebleeds, swelling of the limbs, anemia, and a multitude of other signs. It can be fatal if not treated early and adequately.

Tick Paralysis is somewhat rare. A single imbedded tick can cause the dog (or person) to gradually become immobile and eventually totally paralyzed over several days. Removal of the large, feeding, female tick (*Dermacentor andersoni*) will cause a gradual return to bodily function.

Valley Fever is rare in northern states. In the south and especially the arid southwest, it is much more common. Valley fever is caused by a systemic fungus named *Coccidioides immitus*, and the resulting disease can be fatal. It occurs most commonly in desert regions of the southwestern United States. Wind-borne, microscopic fungal spores are nearly indestructible and remain dormant in the soil for years. Those spores cause disease when they are ingested or inhaled by a receptive host. Upon invasion, the organism springs to life, reproduces rapidly, and may cause a plethora of nonspecific signs. Those signs of infection include lethargy, pain and swelling of various joints, tenderness, lameness, lung involvement that results in respiratory distress, and a variety of other problems. Valley fever can be treated if it is recognized early enough. Unfortunately, it is sometimes tough to diagnose, very difficult to treat, and often requires many months of therapy.

CAUTION

Gasping can be a pathological symptom and should not be totally ignored.

Canine Influenza is reported to be a relatively new canine disease. It was first studied in Florida early in 2004 in racing Greyhounds and has apparently spread to other states. It mimics kennel cough early in the course of the disease but may be fatal if not treated appropriately. In its milder form, respiratory symptoms may be apparent for about three weeks before spontaneous recovery occurs. It spreads rapidly by aerosol from sneezing and coughing, thus canine influenza is often seen where dogs are concentrated (such as dog shows). Racing Greyhounds are at risk as well as those participating in other canine events and other closely kenneled dogs. No vaccine is available at this time, and no spread to humans has been documented. Your veterinarian can send blood samples from suspected dogs to a laboratory for positive identification.

Rabies is a fatal, systemic, neurological disease of all warm blooded animals (including humans). Rabies virus invades the salivary glands of an infected animal and paralyzes its throat. The virus is transmitted from one animal to another through infected saliva and frequently follows being bitten by a rabid animal. Reservoirs are found in wild animals such as coyotes, skunks, raccoons, bats, rats, ferrets, mink, and others. It also occurs in farm animals such as cattle and pets such as dogs and cats. If a human is bitten by a rabid animal, immediate medical treatment is necessary to stop the infection and death.

Arthritis is a potentially debilitating disease that includes joint inflammation. Arthritis might be caused by infection, injury, hereditary diseases, or old age deterioration. It can occur in any joint of the Pug's body, but often it is first recognized in the hips, elbows, or spine. Obesity often exacerbates the condition. It is a progressive ailment that may be treated by a number of oral or injectable anti-inflammatory medications. In some cases, surgery may help. If your old Pug is showing arthritic signs, ask your veterinarian if a glucosamine-chondroitin supplement is indicated. (See the *Pug Senior Citizens* chapter.)

Allergies are associated with ingested food, inhaled particles, or physical contact with allergenic substances. Allergies may cause gastric upsets, or they may be manifested by itching, skin redness, and other topical problems. Allergic reactions can be prevented in many cases by the use of antihistamines. Contact your veterinarian to determine the correct dosage and preferred product. Allergies may also be prevented by desensitizing your Pug, but that technique is costly. Allergy therapy usually entails oral or injectable steroids.

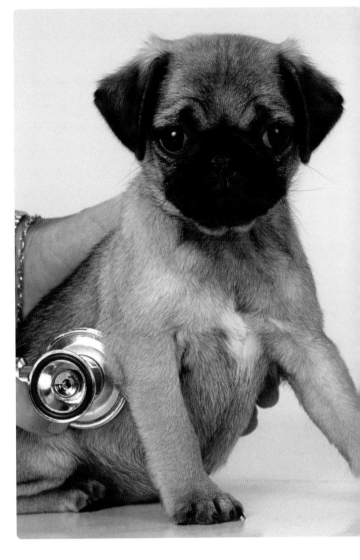

Poisoning may occur from ingesting or contact with many kitchen, garage, or garden chemicals. Poisonous plants are found everywhere. If you fear that your Pug has eaten a toxic plant or chemical, call the National Animal Poison Control Center at (800) 548-2423 or (900) 680-0000, or the ASPCA Poison Control Center at (888) 426-4435.

Hip Dysplasia (CHD) is a hereditary deformity of nearly all breeds of dogs and is much more prominent in giant or large breeds and in hunting breeds. It occasionally is found in small dogs, including Pugs. The problem lies in the ball and socket hip joint, which develops abnormally, becomes arthritic, and worsens throughout life. If your Pug is showing evidence of hip sensitivity and is limping on a hind leg, make an appointment with your veterinarian.

Anal Sac Impaction is signified by Muggs scooting on her bottom. An anal sac is located on each side of the anal opening. They are filled with a foul-smelling, oily secretion that partially empties each time she has a bowel movement. When a piece of dried feces occludes the natural opening and prevents normal drainage, the sac bulges and becomes quite uncomfortable. Muggs then scoots on her bottom, which sometimes opens the pore and the impaction is relieved. If that doesn't work, you can assist by milking out the foul material as described below.

Stand Muggs on a no-slip mat on a table, put on a pair of latex or nitrile gloves (industrial nitrile gloves are cheaper and tougher than most disposable latex gloves), and with one hand, hold her tail out of the way and place a folded piece of toilet paper over the anal area. Press in with your thumb and index finger until you can feel the pea- to marble-sized sacs. Then squeeze the sacs between your thumb and finger, and slowly but firmly milk the sacs' fluid into the toilet paper in the palm of your hand. Clean her anal area, flush the paper, and wash and discard the gloves in the trash. If you haven't the stomach for the procedure, make a trip to your veterinarian.

Parasites

Parasites and their control is more complicated each year. Your local veterinarian knows which parasites are present in your area, how to diagnose infestation, what time of the year to treat, and what products are safest and most effective. Oral or wipe-on products are available that prevent or eliminate several different parasites when administered on a specific time schedule.

Many scams, hoaxes, and antiquated methods of parasite control also exist. Don't attempt to diagnose, treat, or prevent parasites without expert advice. No universally effective worm medication exists. An especially perilous procedure is to worm all puppies, whether or not a parasite infestation has been diagnosed. NOTE: There is no excuse for worming Muggs when she is not infested with those parasites.

Endoparasites
Endoparasites live within your Pug's body at your Pug's expense. They derive their sustenance by living off the waste and blood within her body.

- **Roundworms** grow to rather large dimensions, live in the small intestine, and absorb your Pug's food. They thereby cause nutritional stress, pot belly, and lowered disease resistance. Roundworm eggs pass out with an infested pup's feces and are consumed by other dogs.
- **Hookworms** are microscopic, blood-sucking intestinal parasites that can cause anemia and pain to their hosts. Hookworm eggs pass out of the gut in feces, hatch into larvae, penetrate the skin of susceptible hosts, and migrate through the host's tissues.

- **Tapeworm** is a two-host parasite. An adult tapeworm attaches its head (scolex) to the lining of a dog's intestine, where its segmented body grows and reaches great lengths. Segments break off, pass from the dog's bowel, and stick to a blade of grass or leaf where it is consumed by a secondary host such as a flea or larger creature such as a deer. The segment disintegrates inside the secondary host's intestine and forms cysts containing scolices. Another primary host (dog) consumes the tissues of the secondary host (roadkill venison or flea), which contains the tapeworm cyst.
- **Heartworm** is a threat to all American dogs. An adult heartworm may be many inches long, lives within the heart's chambers or large blood vessels, and produces living larvae which migrate into the host dog's peripheral blood vessels. The presence of heavy heartworm infestation can cause cardiac swelling and can seriously compromise the host's life. When a mosquito sucks blood from an infested dog's vessels, the larvae of the heartworm (*Dirofilaria immitus*) are picked up by the mosquito and are then injected into new canine hosts.

Ectoparasites

These live on and within their host's skin. They are usually diagnosed by skin scrapings or culture and are treated with topical or systemic medication.

- **Mites** are microscopic, eight-legged parasites that burrow beneath and within their host's skin. Several genera of mites cause hair loss, inflammation, itching, and serum oozing. *Cheyletiella*, *Demodex*, *Psoroptes* (a rabbit mite that is occasionally found in dogs), and *Sarcoptes* are identified in skin scrapings that are viewed under a microscope. Ear mites (*Otodectes*) may parasitize Muggs' ear canals and are diagnosed by examining her ear wax under a magnifying glass.

Helpful Hints

Don't waste your cash on dips, sprays, powders, medicated collars, or other devices and drugs that are not labeled for the age and weight of your Pug.

- **Fungus** (*Microsporum* spp.) infestation may be found on your Pug's belly skin and appears as a circular, raised, red lesion; hence its common name is ringworm. It may be treated topically or with oral medication.
- **Fleas** are extremely common, and their control should receive your undivided attention. A flea lives part-time on a host's body and part-time in the host's environment. Infestations are more prevalent in the warm, high-humidity regions of America but are a problem everywhere except, perhaps, in the high mountainous, cooler climates. A flea bites its host and laps the oozing serum. A flea's saliva often causes allergic inflammation and itching. Adult fleas may be found on Muggs' back where you might

HOME BASICS
Tick Removal

To remove a tick, put on a pair of latex or nitrile gloves. Apply alcohol to the hair surrounding the tick, and grasp the tick as close as possible to its host's skin with a pair of blunt tweezers or hemostat forceps. Slowly pull the tick out, using gentle but firm pressure. Don't handle the tick with your bare hands. Drop it into a vial of alcohol. Don't crush it, don't toss it on the ground or into a wastebasket, and don't burn it. After the tick is removed, clean the skin lesion that remains with alcohol or 2 percent hydrogen peroxide twice daily for a few days to prevent infection.

see dozens of them hopping about on her fur. Adult fleas lay eggs, which drop and molt on the ground or floor, where the larvae eat organic material. After additional molts, the adult flea emerges and seeks a viable host, beginning the whole cycle again.

Biological control programs have been devised that involve an application of tiny nematodes (worms) to your backyard. The nematodes consume flea eggs but are harmless to humans and pets. After the nematodes have eaten all the flea eggs, they will die off. If Muggs stays home and the neighbors also use the nematodes, you will be rid of fleas. Other controls involve the use of insect growth-regulator hormones that interfere with the flea's life cycle. Wipe-on products, which are applied to your Pug's skin once a month, are very effective as well.

- **Lice** dwell permanently on the Pug's skin and feed on the blood of the host. They are readily controlled by the use of dips, sprays, or medicated baths. A louse lays its white eggs, called nits, and sticks them on the dog's hair where they can be found with the aid of a magnifying glass.
- **Ticks** can be seen with your naked eye. The female tick buries her head in the host's skin and sucks blood, which causes her body to swell to the size of a grape. The blood-engorged female drops to the ground or carpet and lays thousands of eggs, which hatch and molt twice to become adults. Each of the three life stages of a tick must suck blood from a particular host in order to molt and progress to the next stage. Most ticks require hosts of different species: one for the adult, one for the larva, and one for the nymph. The tick that is most difficult to control is *Rhipcephalus sanguineus*, or brown dog tick, because all stages of that parasite feed on canine blood. Ticks act as vectors for various conditions, such as Lyme disease, tick paralysis, and tick fever.

Genetic Pug Conditions

Hereditary or genetic diseases are unlikely to be found in Pugs from reputable breeders, especially when the breeder has carefully screened the parents. However, some of the most prevalent hereditary conditions are noteworthy to mention.

Anesthesia Danger All Pugs are at risk when general anesthesia by inhalation or injection is used. Often the anesthetic risk far exceeds the procedure for which the anesthetic is administered, even when short-acting agents are used. Anesthetic risk should always be seriously considered when Muggs is scheduled for routine therapeutic procedures such as dentistry, surgery, and some diagnostic techniques. Experience with Pug anesthetic risk should be discussed at the time Muggs' veterinarian is chosen.

Pug Acne This occurs when an affected six-month-old Pug puppy develops typical acne lesions on her face. Those lesions are usually treated by application of 2 percent hydrogen peroxide, and the condition usually runs its course in a month or two. Don't squeeze the pimples because that will cause the acne to spread.

Pug Dog Encephalitis (PDE) PDE is a rare brain inflammation found in some strains of Pugs, the signs of which are head pressing, circling, blindness, and epileptiform seizures. It is a fatal condition with no recognized successful therapy that is seen in a few Pugs between the ages of six months to three years.

Soft Palate Elongation This occurs in many brachycephalic breeds, including Pugs. The palate is longer and thicker than normal. With Muggs' compact airways, the increased length or swelling of these structures may cause difficult breathing. When excited, hot, exercising strenuously, panting, or breathing heavily, the thickened palate is forced into the back of the oral cavity (larynx). A significant amount of air supply to her lungs is shut off, causing dyspnea (shortness of breath). She snorts or gasps, may become anoxic (total deprivation of oxygen), and may collapse. The condition is aggravated by obesity, but soft palate surgery may relieve the problem. The gasping sound is similar to a reverse sneeze, which is usually repeated. Those reverse sneezing episodes will normally stop in a few seconds and should not alarm you. However, they are frightening the first time your Pug experiences them. Appropriate reaction to the situation is to calm Muggs by talking to her, quieting her, and gently rubbing her throat to induce swallowing.

Stenotic Nares This may occur in Muggs and is another brachycephalic problem to watch for. The nasal openings are tiny, the loose skin of the muzzle aggravates the situation, and Muggs breathes through her mouth. That condition is also exacerbated by obesity but may be surgically corrected.

Keratitis Sicca (Dry Eye) This is a condition related to Muggs' prominent globular eye. If the lack of normal tearing is suspected during your in-home exam, report it to your veterinarian immediately. The veterinarian will undoubtedly prescribe an artificial tear preparation that will be used indefinitely, but the good news is your Pug's eyesight will not be compromised if it is treated aggressively.

Pigmentary Keratitis (PK)   PK is another hereditary disease of many breeds, including Pugs. It begins spontaneously without physical cause. Tiny vessels begin to invade the crystal-clear cornea from the limbus (junction of the white of the eye and the cornea). Those blood vessels gradually move across the cornea. They carry with them pigment from the limbus and deposit it in the corneal tissue. If that condition goes untreated, PK can cause total blindness. If it is diagnosed early, it can usually be held in check by use of steroid ointments or drops to the eye. If you suspect this condition in Muggs, make an appointment with your veterinarian.

Trichiasis   This is a hereditary condition of many breeds wherein ingrown eyelashes cause corneal irritation that may be corrected surgically.

Distichiasis   This is genetically transmitted in several breeds. Two rows of eyelashes are present and cause ocular irritation and tearing. Distichiasis can be surgically corrected.

Entropion   This means one or both eyelids roll inward and the lashes irritate the corneas. It can be hereditary and is a developmental eyelid condition of Pugs and others, which can be corrected surgically.

Legg-Perthes   This disease is a hereditary, developmental disease that causes the ball at the upper end of the femur (thigh bone) to gradually degenerate. No prevention or cure is available for this disease, but the pain and lameness can be relieved surgically.

Patellar Luxation (Dislocation)   This is a hereditary condition of many breeds, including the Pug, in which the stifle joint ligaments are weakened, the groove in the upper tibia is too shallow, and the groove is sometimes misaligned to the right or left of center. The kneecap (patella) normally slides up and down in that groove when the stifle joint is flexed. In patellar luxation, the patella slips out of the shallow or misaligned groove and remains there, sometimes locking the flexed joint. An affected Pug will usually skip about on three legs until, eventually, she lies down and extends the leg. The patella may slip back into place, allowing normal leg movement until the patella slips out again. This condition may be corrected surgically.

Collapsed Trachea   This is a less common disease of many small dog breeds. The syndrome begins when a cartilage ring in the trachea is congenitally softer than normal. That soft ring folds, limiting the airway through which the dog breathes. Tracheal collapse is aggravated by obesity and will cause respiratory honking and difficult breathing. Surgical correction is possible. Success depends on several factors, including the number of rings that are affected.

Pug Nutrition

A healthy and happy Pug is a good eater. In fact, Muggs may be the best eater in your family. You should feed the family cat on a short table that Muggs can't reach, because cat food is exceedingly tasty and quite fattening! Everyone in the household should be instructed not to appease Muggs' sitting-up and begging habits. Your intelligent Pug will correctly assume that a treat is a reward for the performance of a trick, and she knows many tricks. Clever little Muggs will stealthily tiptoe from one person to another to beg for table tidbits. She will quickly learn that sitting up, standing on her hind legs, and dancing around and around are only a few tricks that she can perform for a morsel of people food. She will play dead, roll over and over, stand on hind legs, and wave at you by the hour for a tidbit. Don't fall into her trap or you will lose the game, and your wonderful companion will eat herself into obesity.

Breed Truths

Muggs is a small dog. No, she is a tiny lump of winsome mischievousness and it is hard to refuse anything when she begs.

A Pug can charm the groceries right off your table. When given a choice between dog food and people food, Muggs will quickly opt for the latter. If you yield to her choices, she will pay for your imprudent judgment with poor health, dental problems, dietary imbalances, and nutritional deficiencies.

It is nearly impossible to concoct a balanced canine diet in your kitchen. You can learn canine nutritional requirements from a book, but formulation cannot be accomplished with a by-guess-and by-golly technique. The homey saying, "If it is good enough for me, it's good enough for my dog," won't fly. You will very likely be disappointed if you decide to feed Muggs from your table, and your cherished little Pug will be the real loser. Probably the first danger she will face is obesity, but others will soon be encountered.

Often, meat scraps that contain loads of fat and dairy items are unsafe; they can lead to obesity and possibly pancreatic inflammation. Cooked bones are always very dangerous as they can splinter and lacerate the throat and puncture the gastrointestinal tract. Bakery items are risky, and candy can be a serious threat—both will lead to obesity. Just one chocolate bonbon is a hundred times more than Muggs should eat.

Breed Needs

Muggs' daily dietary needs increase when she is under stress associated with rapid growth, illness, or injury.

Pug Dietary Needs

An adult Pug stands a mere 11 or 12 inches tall and weighs about 14 or 15 pounds. In dietary terms, her diminutive size equates to small caloric intake. She needs the best quality of dog food your money can buy, and she needs two or more modest meals daily. She definitely doesn't need small meals between her regular meals.

Muggs has a gourmet palate and an extremely well-developed olfactory (scenting) system. If catered to, she will select foods that she wants. In her mind, well-balanced nutrition means anything that tastes and smells like beefsteak, baked beans, or tuna casserole. You are the alpha member of her family, the boss. It is up to you to read dog food labels, pay attention to

HOME BASICS
Food Facts

- Premium brands of puppy or adult food supply the most reliable nutrition. They are packaged in cans of wet or bags of dry food. They are expensive by the pound, but Muggs' minimal requirements put the cost well within your budget.
- Muggs requires frequent feedings because her metabolic rate is higher than that of large dogs.
- The quantity of food to feed depends on the type (dry or canned) you choose.
- A growing puppy requires at least twice the calories of an adult dog of the same size.
- A dog food package lists the average amounts to feed puppies of different weights, but those figures are only approximate guidelines.
- The National Research Council (NRC) is a governmental body that publishes an excellent, inexpensive booklet containing technical canine nutritional information, which may be purchased by calling 1-800-624-6242.

what you read, and choose appropriately from the plethora of dog foods found on the store shelf.

A dog food containing nutrients that are not digestible may have a colorful label that specifies the total quantity of each nutrient but that doesn't mention bioavailability, the amount of a food ingredient that is digested and actually used for energy. If in doubt, call or write the manufacturer or select another product.

Dogs are not true carnivores; they are omnivores. Their wild progenitors relished the contents of the stomachs of their vegetarian prey. Pugs will live happier and healthier lives when fed both animal and vegetable components because some amino and fatty acids of animal origin are extremely healthful in a Pug's diet. Don't buy a dog food if the first ingredients on the label are of vegetable origin.

Choose a brand and type of dog food that is nutritious, satisfying, and tasty. At the very least, choose a food that is manufactured under the trial guidelines of the American Association of Food Control Officials (AAFCO), a group of veterinary scientists that sets forth standards for canine feeding tests.

An AAFCO imprint on the label is your assurance that the food in the package has been successfully fed to a minimum number of dogs, of certain ages and sizes, for a minimum time period, under controlled conditions. That food is thereby guaranteed by the manufacturers to supply Muggs with total nutrition for her life stage.

FYI: Reading a Label

A dog food label is a legal document that tells you a great deal, providing you know what to look for. By law, every dog food label must identify its ingredients and list them in order of quantity. If soy flour is listed first, the product contains more soy flour than any other ingredient. The National Research Council (NRC) of the National Academy of Sciences reviews scientific data and establishes minimum nutritional requirements for dogs of all ages and sizes under varying circumstances. A dog food that meets the recommendations of the NRC applies only to maintenance requirements. Such a food is adequate for dogs under minimal stress but may be inadequate for growing puppies, performance dogs, or breeding animals.

Feeding Quantity and Frequency

When little Muggs first arrives in your home, she should receive the same number of meals of the same food that she was fed by her breeder. Changing her diet during the first days in a new environment may cause a digestive problem. Don't forget that Muggs is growing every day. Every week, give her a tiny bit more food than you expect her to eat and remove all that is left after 10 minutes. Using that rule of thumb, feed her four times daily until she is three months old, then three times daily until six months of age, and afterward, twice daily for the rest of her life.

Overfeeding Danger

From birth to death, Muggs' growth, health, and physical and mental developments are reflections of her diet. Obesity is seen too often in Pugs. To prevent obesity, buy or borrow a scale, weigh Muggs periodically, and record the date and her weight. As she matures and becomes more active, her metabolism will demand more calories. She will eat more, topping out at around 14 pounds when she reaches one year of age. If she continues to gain weight but is getting no taller, give her smaller meals. Run your fingers over her rib cage. Her ribs should always be palpable but covered with a thin fat layer. Obesity and diabetes mellitus (sugar diabetes) are definitely associated with obesity, and an obese Pug is at risk for many other ailments as well.

Water

Water is essential for life. Muggs needs a constant source of pure, clean, fresh water.

The amount she requires depends on the type of food, ambient (environmental) temperature, activity level, age, and health status. If she eats dry dog food exclusively, she needs more water for proper digestion than if she is fed canned, because dry food contains very little moisture. Her water consumption is lowest if she is young and healthy, normally active, living in a moderate climate, and eating canned dog food, which contains more than 50 percent water. The obvious problem with feeding canned food is paying for all that water!

Commercial Dog Food Types

A dry dog food is usually the cheapest type available and is easiest to store, but it often lacks palatability. Muggs isn't hard to please. In recent years, formulations have bridged the palatability gap.

Canned foods are usually quite palatable, but they may cause urinary frequency due to the diuretic effect of preservatives and seasoning. Canned food contains up to 70 percent water. Meat quality in canned foods may be poor, and some canned foods contain virtually no meat. The quality of contents and prices vary tremendously, and labels reveal very interesting ingredients.

No great advantage is gained by mixing dry foods with canned products except to increase palatability. If you do mix one with the other, choose premium canned foods to mix with premium dry food.

Breed Truths

Muggs is not a picky eater. Virtually no food designed for pets or humans is likely to be rejected by your Pug, but obesity is perhaps the worst enemy of a healthy Pug.

Semi-moist foods that are packed in plastic pouches appear to be ground meat, but they rarely contain any appreciable amount of animal protein. They don't keep as well as canned foods, cost more per pound, and may contain sugars and chemical preservatives that may constitute health risks. Diets of semi-moist products can promote excessive water consumption and frequent urination. They are sometimes incriminated as the cause for certain allergic reactions as well. Further, they may be dangerous for Muggs because of the large amount of water that must be consumed to rehydrate the food once it is eaten.

FYI: Understanding Dog Food Labels

- Amino acids are protein components.
- Calories or KCal refer to the amount of energy contained in a given amount of the food.
- Complete and balanced means that the food can be fed without adding any supplements.
- Crude fat is the amount of animal and plant fat contained.
- Crude protein is the amount of animal and plant protein contained.
- Fatty acids are the components of animal or plant fats.
- Ingredients are always listed in order of largest to smallest amount contained.
- Moisture content is the amount of water contained in the food.
- Puppy foods are specifically formulated for growing puppies and meet the needs of pups from weaning to adulthood without adding any supplements.
- Maintenance rations furnish all the necessary dietary elements for dogs' lives between one year or 18 months of age and upward.
- Stress formulas contain ingredients that are meant to boost the resistance and general health of an injured or ill Pug during the time of an extra nutritional burden. Those formulations contain higher than normal bioavailable nutrients to reduce the total amount of food needed.
- Geriatric diets are formulated for old dogs whose organs are beginning to deteriorate. They are formulated for those Pugs that are not effectively absorbing the nutrients that are present in adult diets and those who need a little extra nutritional help.
- Supplements are additive products such as fatty acids, amino acids, vitamins, minerals, and sometimes enzymes. Those are rarely necessary if Muggs' diet is carefully chosen and fed in appropriate amounts.

Note: Don't feed supplements unless advised to do so by Muggs' health professional. Certain vitamins, such as A and D, may accumulate in her system and become detrimental to her health.

Premium Food

The most expensive dry dog foods available are premium foods, but most of those expensive foods are actually the most economical. Their high nutritional content means you feed less quantity, and their high bioavailability means less waste and smaller volumes of feces produced. You may assume that all premium brands contain superior-quality ingredients and are therefore the most reliable suppliers of excellent canine nutrition. That may be true, but a high price doesn't necessarily reflect premium quality. You must read all labels carefully. Sometimes a premium-brand label is discovered on a formula that does not compare favorably with that of a lower-cost, brand-name product. Some of those well-known, brand-name manufacturers now produce excellent premium-quality foods.

Brand-name Food

Palatability is important, and favorable taste usually increases with the price paid. However, lower-priced brand-name foods may be quite palatable. In many cases, they are nutritionally sound as well. Brand-name foods, those that have been on the market for years, are as reliable as ever. Don't ignore them until after you have read and compared the fine print on all labels. Many brands are upgraded to keep up with the competition in all categories, and they compare well both on the label and in the food bowl.

Generic or House Brands

Generic dog foods are usually priced below all others, although you may find a generic food that compares well with brand-name foods. A seasonal reason may explain that paradox. A dog food may change from one season to another by changing the ingredients' order on the label. For instance, a product may list both corn and beef in the ingredients. It may drop most of the beef from the formula (17 percent protein) and substitute more corn meal (14 percent protein). The ingredient list will be the same and the percent protein will stay nearly the same, but the taste and bioavailability will be vastly different. To put it another way, if the corn (14%) protein is increased in volume and at the same time if the beef (17%) is lowered in volume by just a tad, the percent protein will remain static. Similarly, not all grains contain the same percent of protein. By manipulating the quantity of each ingredient used, protein quantity is changed in the finished dog food product. Chicken has a different protein content as well. Thus, by buying an animal or grain product in season, at a lower price, the dog food cost may remain the same, the formula will remain nearly the same, but the product's taste may differ significantly. The label will tell you why Muggs may find a particular brand very palatable one time and will cast a disappointed look your way when you next buy the same brand.

Treats

Treats are helpful when training Muggs and for offering a little extra love to your companion. Keep them pea-sized. As long as Muggs isn't receiving more than an ounce per day, they're OK. To be sure you're not over-feeding, measure the quantity of her daily treats, and deduct that amount from her daily ration. Better yet, if she responds well to her dry dog food, use a kernel of it for a training reward. If you buy commercial treats, check the ingredients the same as if they were her regular food; they are packaged with the same label requirements as dog foods.

How Much to Feed?

Unfortunately, the directions on a sack of dry maintenance dog food or on a canned food can't be trusted. Those instructions are generic and written to fit average dogs' dietary needs. Muggs isn't average. She is a pig, and her caloric intake should be governed by her physical condition, not a general statement made by someone who

Food Facts to Remember

- Consider the quality of food, not just the price.
- Don't change food without good reason.
- Don't feed your puppy a food that is designated as an "NRC maintenance diet," because it is designed for normal adults and not youths.
- If a label doesn't have an AAFCO declaration, call the toll-free number on the package and ask about feeding trials.
- Call for specific information about a food's source of protein, fat, and carbohydrate if that information does not appear on the label.
- Always buy small bags of food because the nutritional value decreases with storage.

doesn't know her. Feed her slightly less than the package recommendations, and weigh her weekly. If she begins to lose weight, increase her intake, and if she is gaining, cut back a bit. Muggs should be strong, playful, active, mentally alert, curious, and ready for action. If she is frequently lethargic, disinterested, or less energetic than you think is normal, she may be suffering from a nutritional imbalance. If in doubt, ask your veterinarian.

It is not normal for a healthy Pug to leave food in her dish. If she does so, you are probably overfeeding her. She should finish her meal and lick the bowl, but she shouldn't search for more food. If she does, weigh her, palpate her ribs, and consider increasing her intake with the next feeding.

Questions to Ask Yourself Before Breeding

1. Are you planning to breed Muggs because her litter would improve the breed?
2. Has she been faulted by experts on Pug conformation?
3. Has she won acclaim in the show ring?
4. Are you willing to devote countless hours of your time and a great deal of money on show classes, training, and competing against the very best Pugs at dog shows?

Deep Pockets and Genuine Dedication

If your answers to the above questions have been yes, have you considered the costs?

Costs include:

- Testing and proving Muggs' freedom from congenital diseases.
- Proving her conformation, including show entry fees, training, handler's fees, and travel.
- Providing health and dietary care for a brood bitch and her litter.
- Prenatal and post-whelping exams, possible X-ray and ultrasound imaging, as well as potential caesarian section.
- Whelping box, puppy food, and puppy immunizations.
- Time spent cleaning up after a litter for several weeks as well as finding the best homes for puppies.
- Treatment of pyometra or mammary cancer if those conditions should arise, both of which are prevalent in unspayed bitches.

Breeding Your Pug

If you are seriously considering breeding Muggs, be aware that purebred dog breeding is not a lucrative business or avocation. Professional and trustworthy breeders are easily found, but few are driving Rolls Royce vans to dog shows. Raising puppies correctly takes loads of time, a lot of knowledge, and a bundle of cash.

Most competent Pug breeders are truly professional and reputable people whose motives are honorable. They raise Pugs because they love the breed and want to improve it. They raise only a few litters a year. They train and show their dogs against the finest competition in the world. They produce excellent Pug puppies from beautiful dams and winning sires. Those breeders admit that only a small number of their puppies are of show and breeding quality. For that matter, precious few Pugs are literally flawless when compared to the Breed Standard.

Wannabe breeders, amateur and backyard breeders, usually posses neither the knowledge nor the quality of brood stock to be considered reputable Pug breeders. They just fumble along, year after year, producing less-than-

average Pug puppies that are physically and genetically poor specimens. Those less-than-standard Pug pups are sold to unknowing friends, a few of whom also decide to breed, perpetuating the backyard scenario. Pug breeding is fraught with many pitfalls that usually discourage and disappoint those who try it. Muggs is a wonderful family pet, trainable companion, and more fun than a monkey on a stick. Those are the reasons you bought her. Think hard and examine your motive for wanting to breed her.

Overpopulation

Encyclopedic dog information estimates that in America, somewhere between three and four million dogs are euthanized annually. Dr. Bonnie Beaver, an extremely knowledgeable veterinarian, teacher, geneticist, researcher, and behaviorist, wrote in one of her books, "More than surgery is needed to control dog numbers. It may take education of a new generation and regulation of the demand." That statement is echoed by millions of people just like you and me. We should do all we can to control canine overpopulation.

Many thousands of dogs, some of them Pugs, are euthanized every year in state, county, and municipal shelters. Some of those dogs are purchased on impulse. Later, those dogs are untrained and unloved nuisances. They became liabilities through no fault of their own. Such lack of planning and ignorance lead to the destruction of wonderful canine pets that are obtained by well-meaning families. Rejected, unwanted American pets now number in the hundreds of thousands in the United States.

Only potential and responsible dog owners and breeders can control canine overpopulation, which is caused by:

- Impulse buying.
- Owners who obtain dogs and don't have them neutered before they reach reproductive age.
- Those who adopt a dog and fail to train it and teach it manners.
- Those who fail to give their time to the dog.

All dog breeders should employ a neutering policy for all pets sold; legal written contracts can be used to ensure that such a policy is enforced. If you buy and can't keep Muggs for any reason, don't abandon her to the streets, dump her in the pound, or turn her over to animal control. Contact your all-breed club, the Pug club in your area, or the American Pug Club. Many Pug Rescue associations are ready to help you deal with your problem. Ask any breeder or your veterinarian to make suggestions.

Spaying and Castrating (Neutering)

If you are not planning to breed your Pug, it is probably best to spay or castrate. Spaying is a surgical ovariohysterectomy (removal of the ovaries and uterus). Some good reasons to spay a female Pug are

- Spaying before first heat dramatically reduces the incidence of mammary (breast) cancer.
- Spaying prevents pyometra, the most dangerous type of uterine infection.
- Spaying prevents messy three-week estrous (heat) periods that occur twice a year.
- Spaying prevents all possibility of accidental breeding.
- Spaying solves the nuisance problem of male dog attraction.
- Spaying may calm a nervous bitch.
- Spaying does not adversely affect the bitch's trainability, companionship, sense of humor, personality, or temperament.

Castration (neutering) is the surgical removal of both testicles. Reasons for castrating a young male are nearly as important as those for spaying a female.

- A castrated male is often a more stable companion pet.
- Prostate cancer is extremely rare in a castrated male.
- Testicular tumors cannot occur in a castrated male.
- A castrated male is content to stay at home and won't dig under a fence to escape when the neighbor's bitch is in heat.
- Castrating a male does not reduce his trainability, companionship, sense of humor, personality, or temperament.

Spaying a female or castrating a male does not predispose obesity. Pugs get fat for the same reasons that people do; consuming more calories than their metabolism uses. Overfeeding causes most obesity problems, but medical reasons also cause dogs to store excess calories. If Muggs becomes overweight, take her to your veterinarian for diagnosis. If she is in normal health except for fat, manage her nutrition better.

10 Questions About Canine Health

1 **I'm a homeopathy follower and have heard of nosodes that can be used instead of vaccines. What are nosodes and are they safe for dogs?** Nosodes are tissue preparations from diseased animals that are administered to healthy dogs instead of vaccinations. Canine immunology experts warn against use of this immunizing approach because it isn't effective and will fail if challenged by virulent disease-causing agents.

2 **Why is the leptospirosis vaccine not used as much as it formerly was?** In recent years, reports of adverse reactions to various vaccines have nearly stopped those vaccines from being administered. The use of leptospirosis vaccine is an example. Ask Muggs' veterinarian if leptospirosis is prevalent in your locality, and ask if the species of leptospirosis in the vaccine is the same as the lepto species that occurs locally. Also ask if cross-immunity between different lepto species is a factor. Then compare disease risk to vaccination risk.

3 **I am a nurse and want to vaccinate my own pug. Is that safe and where can I obtain vaccine?** Don't administer a vaccination yourself unless you are comfortable with the canine being vaccinated and have had training and experience with canine vaccine administration and with the products being used. If you decide to vaccinate your Pug, consider her age. Study the diseases present locally, the vaccines available, and their potential adverse reactions. Purchase the best products available, and don't buy from unknown Internet distributors. Follow the manufacturer's directions to the letter, and keep your fingers crossed. You might get lucky.

4 **I remember a long time ago, we vaccinated our puppy at five or six weeks old. Why not now?** Some veterinarians embrace early vaccination programs, that is, before eight weeks of age. That plan was proven safe and effective to some degree in the 1980s when parvovirus was rampant across America. Those who received early vaccines suffered much lower mortality rates than other pups. If you're committed to early vaccination, booster vaccinations need to be given at regular intervals, and only the highest quality vaccines should be used.

5 **What are core and non-core vaccines?** Core vaccines are those that are deemed by most authorities to be needed by most dogs in most areas of America. They include canine distemper (CD), infectious canine hepatitis (CAV-2), canine parvovirus (CPV), and rabies. Non-core vaccines are administered to dogs with high risk lifestyles and include canine parainfluenza virus, *Bordetella bronchiseptica* (kennel cough), *Leptospira icterohemorrhagiae* (lepto), *Borrelia burgdorferi* (Lyme disease), *Giardia*, canine coronavirus, and canine dental vaccine.

6 Why shouldn't I feed puppy food to my adult Pug?
Puppy food differs from an adult diet principally in caloric content, in source, quality, and quantity of protein, and in vitamin and mineral content. A puppy requires more calories, highly digestible protein, and carefully balanced vitamin and mineral content to meet the stress of growth, development, and training. Puppy food can sometimes be fed to a young adult without causing harm, but always consult with your veterinarian about the formula of the food in question.

7 Can I feed my Pug free choice? In general, the answer is an emphatic NO! Some dogs eat a dry dog food only in amounts they actually need, or "free choice." That plan is highly unlikely to succeed when feeding a Pug because she will gobble up every morsel of food as soon as it hits her bowl. You should refrain from free choice feeding and give your Pug only regular, measured meals.

8 I've always given my dog table scraps. Are they really bad for my Pug? Leftovers from your table can be dangerous for your Pug for a number of reasons. Sugar or salt content of human foods can cause digestive problems. Leftover milk from your cereal may cause diarrhea. Meat or fish scraps, sweets, and gravies are high-calorie products that can initiate dietary imbalance and may be a primary basis of obesity. Your Pug's digestive system may react violently to seasonings that do not upset your stomach. Table scraps may cause allergies, skin problems, and vitamin and mineral deficiencies.

9 I plan to change my Pug puppy's food. What precautions should I take when doing so? If at any time you don't like the quality of your Pug's diet, wait at least a week before you change. Then for three days, mix about three-fourths of her former food with one-fourth new food. If she has no signs of digestive problems, mix half and half for the next three days. Then mix three-fourths new with one-fourth old for three days, and afterward, a complete change should be tolerated without upset.

10 I've noticed that my veterinarian has some special diets for dogs. Should I be feeding my Pug one of those? Special diet foods are available by prescription from veterinarians or over the counter in stores. One of those foods is specially formulated for normal puppies, and others help control certain conditions such as kidney degeneration, obesity, gastroenteritis, heart disease, and other health problems. Consult your veterinarian before you use one of those foods.

135

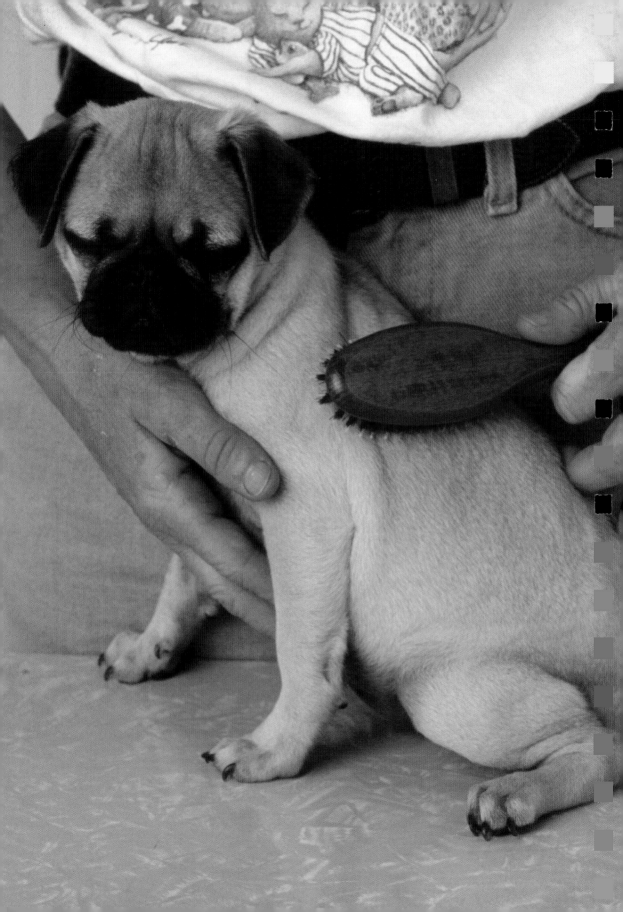

Chapter Seven

Grooming Your Pug

A n essential part of Pug ownership involves grooming. Coat care increases bonding and general health because grooming also includes routine care of eyes, ears, and feet. The 10 minutes spent every few days will be repaid with interest because Muggs enjoys having you fuss over her; she likes the attention. You would be surprised at the number of simple problems that can be averted by regular grooming.

Shedding

Shedding is normal for all canines. A few breeds have coats that give the appearance of not shedding, but they too lose dead hair. You don't find shed hair on the furniture, because those dead hairs are cleverly trapped in their curls. Those curls and the dead hair contained therein are whisked away when the curly Poodle is shaved by a groomer every month.

Helpful Hints

Begin as soon as Muggs joins your family, and continue regular grooming. Make it a habit that you will never regret.

Seasonal shedding is somewhat climate oriented and is related to the amount of daylight afforded. Shedding is related to the quality of your Pug's nutrition as well, and increased outdoor exercise seems to slow down excessive shedding.

Some breeds simply shed more than others. Muggs is a generous little companion that loves to share her coat with her family. Double coats tend to shed more noticeably than single coats, and a fawn Pug has a double coat. Muggs' shedding propensity is perhaps the foremost flaw in this charming little companion's physical makeup. Soft, short hairs manage to work into all fabrics that touch Muggs. Early in your relationship, you will hang a tape-style lint remover in every closet.

Shedding is the bane of Pugs. To minimize it from becoming a super problem, comb and brush Muggs every time you can, but no less that three or four times a week.

Because brushing and grooming are a vital part of Pug ownership, you should consider setting up a corner of the house to devote to that endeavor. Visit a grooming parlor and look at a professional groomer's table. You will see a sturdy table with a bent rod, shaped like an inverted "L," affixed to one end and a loop of soft cord hanging over the table from the horizontal end of the rod. The table is covered with a non-slip rubber mat that is easily removed for cleaning. Collapsible metal grooming tables are available at pet supply stores, but they are expensive ($30 to $100). Much cheaper ones are often available at thrift shops.

Combing and Brushing

A Pug's short coat is cared for by simply brushing. Pugs do admittedly have flyaway hair that can be time consuming. A grooming glove is a blessing to a Pug owner who likes to pet Muggs but doesn't like brushing. Grooming gloves take the "brush" out of brushing. A few minutes of frequent, intense petting with a grooming glove will make shedding manageable. A monthly or semi-monthly bath will make it even more governable. Some shampoos are designed to help retain healthy coats. A high quality diet is critical. Some veterinarians recommend vitamin E and fatty acid supplements that are formulated to improve the nature and texture of coats and help reduce shedding. Regular outdoor exercise is also extremely important to a healthy coat.

HOME BASICS
Preventive Action Will Minimize Shedding

- Spend at least three or four short sessions a week with Muggs and her fine-toothed comb and brush or grooming glove.
- End each quick grooming session by wiping her down with a lightly dampened chamois leather or piece of velvet.
- Buy the best quality dog food available, and don't feed table scraps.
- Ask your veterinarian if a fatty acid and vitamin E supplement may help reduce shedding.
- Buy fawn colored furniture and carpet, and try not to wear dark clothing.

Muggs should be acclimated for more intense grooming while still a pup. When you first bring Muggs home, or at least while she is still a puppy, stand her on your grooming table, slip the leash loop over her head, and talk to her in quiet and reassuring tones. Pet her and rub her body all over with a grooming glove to accustom her to grooming in general. When she sits down, gently lift her bottom and continue petting and rubbing. After three or four minutes on the table, she should relax. When she does, pet her for another minute, then stop, remove the loop, give her a tiny tidbit, tell her what a good dog she is, and set her on the floor. If you repeat that exercise several times a day for a week, she will quickly learn to expect it and won't fight the idea when real grooming starts.

For routine grooming, you'll need a fine comb ($5), bristle brush ($4), and grooming glove ($3.50) or slicker pad ($5). A grooming glove is made of cotton covered with little dots of soft, plastic material, which will gently remove loose hair from her coat. It is highly efficient, and everybody likes the idea of petting Muggs with or without a gloved hand.

If Muggs runs through a puddle and gets wet and muddy, towel her dry, and then set her on the grooming table. If you prefer, a hair dryer set on low heat may be used to dry the mud on her coat. Her short coat lies flat. When dry, the dirt can be combed out with a stainless steel, fine-toothed comb. A quick combing also loosens the undercoat. After combing, brush her with a bristle brush to remove the remainder of dried mud, and use your grooming glove or slicker pad to remove loose hair.

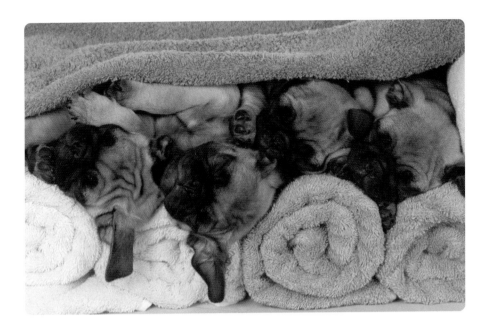

Bathing

Some Pugs develop very little body odor if they are exposed to the sunshine and fresh air daily, in which case, frequent bathing is unnecessary. Bathing helps remove some loose hair. If Muggs rolls in something nasty or if she develops bad body odor for any reason, a bath is in order.

Before bathing, comb and brush Muggs until most of the flyaway hair is gone. Pull a cotton ball in half, twist each half tightly, and work a twist gently into each ear canal. Squeeze a tiny amount of petroleum jelly onto her corneas at the lateral (outside) corner of each eye. It will melt and spread over the cornea to protect her sensitive eyes from shampoo.

Breed Truths

Bathing frequency depends on need, but you shouldn't bathe your Pug more often than every two weeks.

Place a rubber mat in the tub or sink, and fill with about 4 inches of tepid water. Stand Muggs inside the tub. With the shower hose, or if one isn't available, with a cupped hand, dip water and soak her coat. Squirt a modest amount of a good canine shampoo onto her back, neck, abdomen, and rump. Rub briskly. Pick up each foot and leg, and shampoo her tail. Work the shampoo into a lather with your fingers or a shampoo mitt.

Don't shampoo her face. After shampooing her body, rinse the lather off with the shower hose. Dampen a washcloth or soft sponge with clean, warm water. Use the damp washcloth to clean her face and facial wrinkles. Take extra precautions to rinse all wrinkles.

CHECKLIST

Bathing Necessities

- ✔ Cotton balls
- ✔ Tube of sterile petroleum jelly to protect her eyes ($2)
- ✔ Laundry tub or kitchen sink
- ✔ Rubber shower or sink mat ($4)
- ✔ Handheld shower-hose attachment ($8)

- ✔ Canine shampoo ($6–$8)
- ✔ Shampoo mitt ($6) (Optional)
- ✔ A few large towels
- ✔ Washcloth or soft sponge
- ✔ Handheld hair dryer (Optional)

Dry Muggs with a bath towel, taking care to dry wrinkles thoroughly. If bathing in inclement weather, you might need to finish her dry cycle with a handheld hair dyer, turned on low heat and low power.

Muggs' wrinkles are quite susceptible to infection if they are left damp after bathing.

Nail Care

Carpet and soft lawns cause very little nail wear. If she spends the majority of time on those surfaces, her nails may need trimming once a week. If you routinely take her walking on concrete sidewalks or asphalt trails, her nails may require trimming once a month or less.

Helpful Hints

Muggs' nails may need care frequently or only occasionally, depending upon the surfaces on which she spends the most time.

Begin trimming Muggs' nails when she is two- or three-months old. Her first few weeks with you is a training period during which you should routinely snip off the nail tips once a week. Cut only the tips because you do not want to risk causing pain and bleeding by getting a nail too short. From youth until old age, her nails should be quickly examined every time she is groomed and should be trimmed when necessary. As Muggs ages and becomes less active, she will undoubtedly require more frequent nail care. If you see her chewing her nails or hear her nails clicking on the tile, they need attention.

Nail Trimming

Muggs' toenail is a horny, layered structure that grows outward and downward from the last digit of each toe. The quick or nail bed is very sensitive and contains several tiny blood vessels and sensory nerves. Pug nails are black, and the delineation between nail bed and insensitive nail is nearly

CHECKLIST

Nail Trimming Needs

✔ Sharp, well-made nail trimmers. Do not buy a bargain brand. Two varieties are found in pet supply stores, a guillotine-type ($6) and a scissor-type ($8). Many Pug owners prefer the scissor-type, but either will perform the task quite nicely.

✔ A styptic shaving stick from the drugstore ($2.50) or styptic liquid ($10) from a pet supply store.

✔ Cotton swabs.

✔ A helper to hold your Pug puppy quiet while you are trimming the nails.

Note: A canine nail file available at pet supply stores ($3.50) may be used with excellent success instead of a nail trimmer.

impossible to see. If cut too deeply, pain and bleeding result. If toenails are trimmed regularly, the quick will remain significantly behind the tip of the nail. If nails are not worn off or trimmed, the quick gradually grows toward the tip of the nail.

Small wooden sticks coated with silver nitrate solution are best for stopping nail bleeding and are usually available from veterinarians, pet supply stores, or pharmacies. Numerous other blood stoppers are available as well, including a styptic shaving stick, which is the least expensive. Groomers often drag the bleeding nail across, digging it deeply into, a bar of soap. After stopping the bleeding, put Muggs in her crate or pen for an hour to prevent recurrence.

Helpful Hints

A pinch of dry cornstarch or flour pressed to the bleeding nail usually will stop minor nail hemorrhage.

No special training is required, but don't begin the project unless you are committed to finishing it correctly. If she squirms and whines, speak gently, assuring her that she isn't being sacrificed. Proceed with the task, following the directions carefully. Nail trimming takes a steady hand and an easygoing technique. It is easy to cut a little too deeply, but a few drops of blood do not constitute an emergency. Have your styptic products at hand and hope you won't need them.

- Place Muggs on a table covered with a bathtub mat.
- With your helper steadying her, pick up a foot and grip it in your left hand, not too tightly but with authority and tightly enough to prevent withdrawal.
- Spread her toes with slight pressure from the thumb of your left hand.

- Examine the underside of the nail under a bright light. Her toenail appears somewhat like a slightly curved letter "V" lying on its side. The pointed tip of the "V" is hollow, and the base of the "V" is solid and sensitive.
- Start at the tip and snip off a thin slice of nail. Then snip another slice. Closely watch the cross-section of each slice as you proceed.
- In the first slice, the underside of the nail is hollow. As you continue to snip toward her toe, each slice will become more solid. When you near the quick, the slice is nearly filled. Stop trimming at that point. One more slice and the nail will bleed.

If you accidentally cut into the quick and Muggs cries out and yanks her foot away, don't despair. No permanent damage will result, and Muggs will forgive you if you promise to try not to repeat the error. Don't panic or cry out. If you get excited, she will recognize your discomfort and fidget even more. Instead, catch hold of the injured foot, locate the bleeding nail, and apply a moderate amount of digital pressure to the toe to stop the bleeding.

With your free hand, apply a styptic stick to the bleeding nail for a minute or two. (If you are using powder, dampen a cotton

Helpful Hints

A variable-speed hand grinding tool is an excellent alternative to old-fashioned nail trimming. To use, put a sandpaper wheel on the tool, and begin grinding the nail tip using a moderate speed, with the sandpaper wheel held lightly against the nail. It is painless. If the buzz of the tool can be tolerated by Muggs, it is quite easy to keep the nails under control. Stop often to be sure you aren't getting too close to the quick!

143

swab, roll the swab in the powder, and hold it to the bleeding nail.) The hemorrhage will stop, and you can proceed with the nail trimming. If it continues to bleed, repeat the treatment.

Dental Care

Muggs loves to eat, but she doesn't use toothpicks, floss, or a toothbrush. Cleaning Muggs' teeth is another program that you should start during her first few weeks in your home. Her baby teeth are still in place. Obviously they are strong and clean, but routine brushing at an early age will accustom her to that grooming task, which will be better accepted later.

Canine preventive dentistry can stop periodontitis (gum inflammation), which has long been neglected by owners. Untold numbers of small dogs are anesthetized to clean their teeth and extract those that are loose, covered with plaque and tartar, and beyond saving. Many older canines' health problems, such as nephritis (degenerative kidney disease), cardiac diseases, arthritis, and other conditions are related to periodontitis. Food particles gather between teeth, and oral bacteria grow in this warm, moist environment. Those germs eventually infect the soft gum tissues. The infection travels through the bloodstream to various susceptible organs.

Encourage Muggs to chew on firm objects such as nylon bones and hard-twisted rawhide sticks, dry dog food, and hard biscuits. Today, pet supply stores prominently display "dental chews" specifically designed to increase the tooth action and help remove or prevent plaque. Owners are beginning

HOME BASICS
Tooth Brushing

- Only the outside surface of the teeth need to be brushed.
- You do not need to pry open Muggs' mouth.
- Use either a finger-brush ($3–$5) that slips over your index finger or a standard canine toothbrush ($4.50).
- Always use canine toothpaste ($4–$6), in flavors approved by Muggs. Mint-flavored, human toothpaste should not be substituted, and its use may defeat the entire brushing program. Dog toothpaste tastes like meat; human toothpaste tastes like peppermint, which is not acceptable to Pugs.
- Apply a short ribbon of toothpaste to the finger-brush (or toothbrush), slip the brush between her lips, and brush the incisors, canines, and molars. Be quick and thorough.
- Muggs will become accustomed to this routine in a few days, and the flavor of the toothpaste will encourage her participation. Tooth brushing should definitely become a part of Muggs' routine grooming sessions.

to recognize that chewing firm objects is an important part of canine preventive dentistry, but that isn't enough. For many years, veterinarians have suggested wrapping a bit of gauze tightly around an index finger, dampening it with 2 percent hydrogen peroxide, and scrubbing the surface of the teeth. That technique works well, but most dogs hate it! The peroxide foams, it tastes horrible, and many dogs will not tolerate such preventive therapy.

More recently, preventive oral hygiene has made strides, and canine tooth brushing is now recognized as a beneficial part of your companion's grooming. Brushing is an easily accomplished task that takes only a minute or two. When employed several times a week, it possibly prevents tartar and plaque formation. Sound teeth reduce bad breath and minimize the need for professional cleaning and extractions. Brushing makes good sense because you are avoiding veterinary fees and thereby saving dollars in the bargain. A new periodontitis vaccine discussed in the *Pug Health and Nutrition* chapter may prove to be a significant additional tool for infected gums. However, only brushing will remove existing debris from between teeth, prevent discoloration, and stop tartar from beginning to form.

Wrinkle Care

Much like tooth brushing, wrinkle care should be a part of regular grooming. Much of Muggs' clown-like appearance and personality are her distinctive facial features, those muzzle wrinkles, and perhaps an extra one found on the hindmost part of her back. Those distinctive skin wrinkles may be a mixed blessing. They sometimes trap moisture, become inflamed and promote bacterial infection, which may cause inflammation, scratching, and bad odor.

Preventive wrinkle care takes only a few seconds. Use a dry cotton swab, and run it down into each wrinkle. If moisture or bad odors are found, refer to the paragraphs in the *Pug Health and Nutrition* chapter that deal with treatment of those problems.

Eye and Ear Care

Muggs' large, prominent eyes and the wrinkles below them are very important and should be checked daily. Normal tearing carries moisture to Muggs' wrinkles. That moisture should be cleaned from her muzzle daily with a moist cotton ball and dried with another cotton ball. Moisture may attract dust and dirt and then result in conjunctivitis. If you note excessive tearing or any yellow or orange mucoid eye drainage, call Muggs' veterinarian.

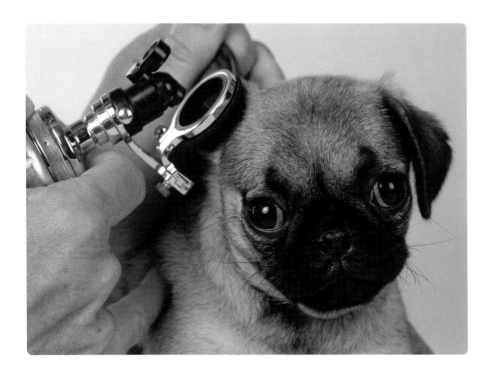

Routine ear canal care is another facet of grooming. At least once a week, pick up each of Muggs' ears and sniff carefully. A musty odor may be an indication of excess wax formation that you can clean with a cotton ball lightly moistened with hydrogen peroxide. The peroxide will dissolve the wax, and her head shaking afterward will cause the wax to be expelled from the canal. Clean the wax off her coat with a dry cotton ball or paper towel, and remember to check her ears closely during your next grooming session.

CAUTION

Under no circumstances should you clean your Pug's ears by inserting a cotton swab into the canal.

Leg and Body Exam

Pick up and examine each foot for pad abnormalities, and be sure she hasn't picked up a burr or grass seed in the hair between her toes. Run your hand up and down her leg and across her belly and chest to check for skin tumors or the presence of parasites such as ticks. Quickly look at her anus and genital area for evidence of any problems located there. Set Muggs on the floor, tell her what a good dog she is, and treat her to a morsel from your pocket.

Chapter Eight

Pug Senior Citizens

Small dogs live longer than big dogs. That's a rule of thumb that usually applies but may not always be totally correct. A Pugs' life expectancy is influenced by many factors that are discussed throughout this book. Muggs isn't the tiniest dog in town, but she is rather small. With good care, she will probably be with you until she reaches a ripe old age. You are committed to providing her grooming and the best nutrition and preventive health care, so you should expect to have your partner with you for more than a dozen years.

Age-related Changes

A logical method for equating a Pug's life to that of a human is to consider the first year of a dog's life equal to 21 human years and each year thereafter equal to 4 human years. By that calculation, a 15-year-old Pug would be equal to a 77-year-old human. That formula may be nearer to correct than other estimations, such as the time-honored one-to-seven, wherein a 15-year old Pug would equate to a 105-year old human. Any calculation may err when extraneous factors enter into the formula, such as health care, size, exercise, and nutrition.

If we accept that human old age begins at 65, then a Pug's senior state starts at about 12. A small, healthy, well-cared-for dog, like Muggs, may live well beyond 15 years. After she has been a member of your family for about 9 years, she will probably show aging signs. Her black muzzle will gradually sprout gray hair, and she will begin to lose some of her pep and sharpness. She'll play with her toys less and less and will prefer to seek a place in the sun where she can nap. She will still be alert, responsive, and your very best friend.

Old Muggs trusts you explicitly, and you have always been there for her. You want to prolong her comfortable life as long as possible. Recognize that an old friend deserves your most conscientious attention in her declining years, but what more can you do?

- Purchase a retractable leash so that when Muggs wants to meander on her walks, you can let her wander a bit and yet keep her from harm.
- Remember that old dogs cherish creature comforts such as warmth and loving hands.
- Groom Muggs for shorter periods of time but more frequently.
- Take her on short walks on smooth, level surfaces.
- Trim her nails more frequently because they are not wearing off.
- Increase the frequency of her professional physical exams.
- Check her breath and teeth no less than every two weeks.
- Be careful when combing because she may have a few small skin tumors.
- Be aware that arthritis is an old Pug's major problem, and watch for limping and slow rising.
- Watch for changes in appetite and eliminations.

Arthritic Joints

Arthritic symptoms usually begin slowly and almost without visible notice, so it is important that you monitor Muggs' activities very closely. Arthritis is fairly common in old Pugs and is signaled by Muggs' slowing down and taking longer to rise from a lying or sitting position. She may walk with a slight limp when she first gets up in the morning. She may wince when you are grooming her. Playtime activities continue but at a more modest pace and for a more limited time. When you observe those signs, ask your veterinarian to prescribe an anti-inflammatory drug for her. If you buy an anti-inflammatory drug from a pharmacy, ask Muggs' veterinarian if it is safe and what dosage to use. If a blood screen was done on your last visit, it will tell the veterinarian what medications can be used that won't compromise her organ health.

Meanwhile, you can ease Muggs' comfort considerably by adjusting her walks. A brief walk in the neighborhood will let her know that she is still part of the family, but it won't fatigue her or aggravate her arthritic joints.

If she has steps to climb to the back porch, build a little ramp that she can handle more easily than the stairs. If that is not practical, pick up and carry Muggs. She will appreciate the ride, and you probably will earn a special kiss on the chin.

Note her bodily actions as she performs tricks. Often an arthritic Pug will continue her clownish activities even if it hurts. Muggs will sit up, stand up on her hind legs, and dance but with less enthusiasm. If a stunt causes her pain, don't ask her to perform, although she may insist, especially if anti-inflammatory medication is being used.

Weight

Her veterinarian may weigh Muggs and announce that she isn't obese but is a bit overweight. Although she only gained 2 pounds since her last exam, the doctor may dwell on that seemingly tiny weight gain. The veterinarian will explain that Muggs weighed 15 pounds on her last visit but now she's up to 17 pounds. That means she gained 13 percent during the last six months, which would be equal to a gain of 21 pounds for a 170 pound man. The doctor may tell you that weight gain may be related to disease. Probably Muggs feels better because of the anti-inflammatory medication and is simply getting too many snacks and too little exercise. The veterinarian may advise you to take her for more short walks, stop all people-food snacks, give her only a few treats a day, and reduce each meal by a tablespoonful. Just to be safe, the clinician may take another blood sample to rule out diabetes and other metabolic diseases. Normal test results means no further changes are needed.

Breed Truths

A majority of Pugs past the age of eight or nine are overweight.

Dental Problems

Tartar may build up on Muggs' teeth if you haven't kept up with her dental hygiene program. Aging may result in less chewing on her nylon bones and rawhide sticks. As that process continues, she will eat slower, crave fewer tidbits, roll food around in her mouth before swallowing, and develop foul smelling breath. Those are all clinical signs of dental plaque, periodontitis, or an abscessed tooth.

A dental examination may reveal that some teeth are loose, may require extraction, and if allowed to progress, may lead to kidney or cardiac disease. Extractions may be needed, which must be done under general anesthesia. If the veterinarian decides that Muggs is in good condition and after discussing the risks of general anesthesia, he or she will probably decide to do a health screen to check out her organ health. If all are in acceptable ranges, Muggs will no doubt undergo dentistry under a general anesthesia a day or two later, and you will no doubt reinstate your home dental hygiene.

Breed Needs

Professional Physical Examinations

Sometime after middle age (about eight), geriatric exams become important.

Consult with your veterinarian when Muggs reaches that age, and follow his or her advice about her need for more frequent well-dog health care examinations. Those exams may include blood tests to reveal kidney, liver, and other organ health. Veterinarians often offer a geriatric profile screening test that isn't prohibitively expensive and may indicate early problems before they cause outward symptoms.

Urinary Incontinence

You may notice that her urine is quite clear and looks like tap water. She may drink much more water than she did a year ago. Aging may bring on incontinence wherein Muggs frequently leaves a small wet spot on the floor or a trace of urine on her blanket. Later, when she wakes after a nap, the leakage may become more significant. She may wake you up twice each night for a trip outside. Your veterinarian will probably suggest a urinalysis and a blood test to detect kidney malfunction, diabetes, or a bladder infection. The tests may reveal that her urine is very dilute and contains no sugar but may also indicate that Muggs is suffering from early stage renal (kidney) degeneration.

You can compensate for some of those changes by feeding her a special kidney-diet food. You will also need to prepare your home. Visit a thrift shop and buy several soft, cotton, rubber-backed bath mats, and place them in her favorite napping places. Set out three more small dishes of water around the house to encourage her to drink all she wants. You can almost hear her thanking you for this. She will love the kidney diet, drink more water, and have better urinary control. In less than a month, she will seem more at ease and perhaps have an increased interest in life!

Following your veterinarian's advice, feed her small, warmed quantities of the special diet three times daily. Stop her people-food snacks, and limit her treats. Muggs will get excited with the smell that comes from the warm kidney diet. You will notice she has lost a few ounces since beginning the new diet and is more content.

Cataracts and Deafness

Muggs' eyesight may fail as she grows older. It will be obvious, because she will often act disoriented when she wakes and bump into furniture that you have moved from its original location. She will appreciate having every chair and table remain in the same place it always was. Your veterinarian probably will tell you that her impending blindness is caused by nuclear sclerosis or senile cataracts, which is opacity of the lens of the eye. He may tell you that her vision is only about 10 percent of normal, and you may discuss cataract surgery. However, her age, deteriorating general condition, risk of anesthesia, and lack of any pain or discomfort discourage such surgery. Besides, she is coping with the vision loss fairly well and seems comfortable most of the time. Her hearing may be diminished as well, and she probably can tell where you are by the vibrations from your walking. The veterinarian may suggest that you stomp when you approach and take care not to startle her by picking her up while she is asleep.

Cognitive Dysfunction

Muggs is now a very old lady who needs assisted living accommodations. She may appear confused occasionally. At 17 years of age she will sometimes defecate on the floor and then act bewildered by what she has done. Your veterinarian will tell you that these signs are the result of a condition known as cognitive dysfunction, which is similar to senile dementia in humans. You can't stop the progress of this condition, and it will gradually become more apparent. Your veterinarian will probably tell you that these signs are the beginning of the end and her life is drawing rapidly to a close. You will soon need to say good-bye to your dear companion.

Saying Good-bye

You can assist Muggs and compensate for many of her old-age changes. Sooner or later she will stop eating, lose all bladder and bowel control, and wander about aimlessly most of the time. She won't remember where the bathmats are and will lie down anywhere. She may whine periodically, stop and stare at the wall for several minutes, and drop to the floor, whether she is on tile or carpet. She will often need someone's help to get up and not even sniff at the urine she leaves behind. Muggs will trip and fall several times a day, and you will perceive that she is begging you to do something. You are her benefactor and have been for these 17 years, and so you may refuse to see her in this condition. The past few weeks will have been extremely difficult for both of you. Her kind veterinarian will suggest that now is the time to give her up.

   You know the decision you must make but ask, "Will she soon die in her sleep?" You already know the answer and think about her life, the joy she has brought to your family, and hesitate. The veterinarian says she will soon die and often an old dog's life does not end easily. Muggs may fall from the porch and break her brittle old bones. She might choke on food and convulse. She has begun to lose weight and will soon be a walking skeleton. She eats less and less, and you are afraid she will starve herself, another horrible eventuality.

Euthanasia is your only humane choice. Your sympathetic veterinarian may agree to come to your home to administer the fatal injection into Muggs' vein. You sit on the rug beside Muggs, stroke her gray old head, and speak to her under your breath as she drifts away without fear or apprehension. Her life ends in familiar surroundings, and she feels nothing

but a slight prick of a needle. In a few seconds her heart stops, and a stethoscope tells the doctor that Muggs is gone. You bury her body in the tiny grave in your backyard, where she played in her youth, and buy a healthy young tree to plant over her as a memorial to her life.

Picking Up the Pieces

Now it is all over, or is it? Muggs was a living being, not a possession that you will easily forget. She was a funny, mischievous clown that loved you and your family, and that love will be remembered for many years to come. Her infectious good humor, playfulness, and all her silly idiosyncrasies will always be with you. Who will ever take her place? What will fill the void in your heart?

No magic words will compensate Pug families for their loss when it is time to euthanize a companion of many years. Don't even try to forget your old pal. Allow her unique personality to live on. Dwell on the happy times Muggs brought to your lives, and not on your loss. Remember Muggs in her prime, racing about the yard, playing with the children, woofing at the mail carrier, and quietly growling at her stuffed bear as she tossed it in the air.

If you believe that discussing your grief will help you cope, obtain the name of a support group from your veterinarian. Don't hurry to find another companion. After an appropriate time has passed, don't be reluctant to obtain another pet. You will know when the time is right, but you will never find a clone for Muggs. She was a singular individual. Your next Pug will be just as unique as she was but different and as clownish in her own way.

Resources

Books

Alderton, David. *Dogs*, London, UK: Dorling Kindersley Limited, 1993.

American Kennel Club. *The Complete Dog Book*, 18th Edition, New York, NY: Simon & Schuster Macmillan Company, 1992.

Beaver, Bonnie V. *Canine Behavior*, Philadelphia, PA: W. B. Saunders Company, 1999.

Clark, Ross D and Stainer, Joan R., *Medical & Genetic Aspects of Purebred Dogs*, St. Simons Island, GA: Forum Publications, Inc., 1994.

Coile, Caroline D. *Encyclopedia of Dog Breeds*, Hauppauge, NY: Barron's Educational Series, Inc., 1998.

Davis, Henry P., *The Modern Dog Encyclopedia*, Harrisburg, PA: The Stackpole Company, 1956.

Rice, Dan F., D.V.M., *Small Dog Breeds*, Hauppauge, NY: Barron's Educational Series, Inc., 2002.

Veerhoef-Verhallen, Esther J. J., *Encyclopaedia of Dogs*, The Netherlands: Rebo Productions, Lisse, 1996.

Von der Leyen, translated by Kimber, Rita and Robert. *Illustrated Guide to 140 Dog Breeds*, Hauppauge, NY: Barron's Educational Series, Inc., 2000.

Yamazaki, Tetsu and Kojima, Toyoharu. *Legacy of the Dog*, San Francisco, CA: Chronicle Books, 1995.

Organizations

The Pug Dog Club of America
www.pugs.org

American Kennel Club
www.akc.org

The Delta Society
www.deltasociety.org

Orthopedic Foundations for Animals
offa.org/hipinfo.html

Canine Eye Registration Foundation
vmdb.org/cerf.html

Canine Freestyle Dancing
www.canine-freestyle.org

Therapy Dogs Inc.
www.therapydogs.com

Wikipedia Internet Encyclopedia
en.wikipedia.org

Index

THE TEAM BEHIND THE *TRAIN YOUR DOG* DVD

Host **Nicole Wilde** is a certified Pet Dog Trainer and internationally recognized author and lecturer. Her books include *So You Want to be a Dog Trainer* and *Help for Your Fearful Dog* (Phantom Publishing). In addition to working with dogs, Nicole has been working with wolves and wolf hybrids for over fifteen years and is considered an expert in the field.

Host **Laura Bourhenne** is a Professional Member of the Association of Pet Dog Trainers and holds a degree in Exotic Animal Training. She has trained many species of animals including several species of primates, birds of prey, and many more. Laura is striving to enrich the lives of pets by training and educating the people they live with.

Director **Leo Zahn** is an award winning director/cinematographer/editor of television commercials, movies, and documentaries. He has directed and edited more than a dozen instructional DVDs through the Picture Company, a subsidiary of Picture Palace, Inc., based in Los Angeles.